JAVIER MARTÍNEZ-TORRÓN

Anglo-American Law and Canon Law

Comparative Studies
in Continental and Anglo-American Legal History
Vergleichende Untersuchungen zur kontinentaleuropäischen
und anglo-amerikanischen Rechtsgeschichte

Herausgegeben von

Helmut Coing, Richard Helmholz, Knut Wolfgang Nörr
und Reinhard Zimmermann

Band 18

Anglo-American Law and Canon Law

Canonical Roots of the Common Law Tradition

By

Javier Martínez-Torrón

Duncker & Humblot · Berlin

Die Deutsche Bibliothek – CIP-Einheitsaufnahme

Martínez-Torrón, Javier:
Anglo-American law and canon law : canonical roots of the common law tradition / by Javier Martínez-Torrón. – Berlin : Duncker und Humblot, 1998
(Comparative studies in continental and Anglo-American legal history ; Bd. 18)
ISBN 3-428-09414-X

Fotoprint: Berliner Buchdruckerei Union GmH, Berlin
Printed in Germany

ISSN 0935-1167
ISBN 3-428-09414-X

Gedruckt auf alterungsbeständigem (säurefreiem) Papier
entsprechend ISO 9706 ♾

"Upon what I said in relation to our Court of Justice, his Majesty desired to be satisfied in several points: and this I was the better able to do, having been formerly almost ruined by a long suit in Chancery […]. He asked […] Whether party, in religion or politics, were observed to be of any weight in the scale of justice. Whether those pleading orators were persons educated in the general knowledge of equity, or only in provincial, national and other local customs. Whether they or their judges had any part in penning those laws, which they assumed the liberty of interpreting and glossing upon at their pleasure."

(Jonathan Swift, *Gulliver's Travels*, part two, chapter VI)

To my wife Lorena,
and to my sons Javier and Guillermo

Preface

This book, written by a young Spaniard of energy and ability, deals with a subject of continued interest to English historians and indeed to students of comparative legal history more generally. He seeks to answer the question of whether the medieval *ius commune*, the amalgam of Roman and canon law that governed European legal education and influenced legal practice for so long, exercised any substantial and sustained influence on the development of Anglo-American law. He finds that it did. The canon law in particular played an important role in the development of several parts of English law. It is an honor to be asked to contribute a Preface to this worthwhile endeavor, for the work has several strengths that are too often missing from discussions of the subject, including my own.

The most remarkable of these strengths is that the author is able to approach the subject with a more thorough grounding in Continental law than is possible for most English legal historians. He finds parallels, connections, and distinctions that are harder for those whose education has been in the history of the common law to see. Although he is familiar with the materials of the English common law, he is not confined by them. His discussion of legal maxims and the *Regulae* of the canonical and civilian traditions is particularly illuminating on this score. Not that he is the first Continental scholar to approach this subject. Our knowledge of the thirteenth century treatise on English law ascribed to Henry Bracton was long ago enriched by contributions by Carl Güterbock, Hermann Kantorowicz, and Fritz Schulz. Martínez-Torrón incorporates their insights and adds his own, showing that Bracton approached legal problems from a juridical perspective that was common to his time, one that was shared by jurists on the other side of the English Channel.

Beyond this Continental perspective, this book approaches the subject in a systematic way that has too often been lacking in treatments of this subject. Professor Charles Donahue once perceptively pointed out that the question of whether there has been influence of Roman and canon laws on English common law was reminiscent of the old story of the blind man and the elephant. Since the old man could touch only a small part of the elephant at one time, his description of the whole depended on which part he happened to be touching at the moment. The story illustrates the danger of making large generalizations from what may be isolated examples. Martínez-Torrón has not fallen into this trap. He has read widely. He treats the institutional history of England's courts system and also takes up many areas of private law, procedural law, and criminal law. His book contains useful and careful excursions into constitutional theory. He has touched as many parts of the elephant as he could.

Finally, the book takes English law as a whole. The author's attentions are not focused upon the royal courts alone. He does deal with the Courts of King's Bench and the Common Pleas and with the assizes that depended upon them. But he also makes room for the Court of Chancery, Admiralty jurisdiction, the ecclesiastical tribunals, and some of the more minor courts of equity. This is only realistic. English law cannot be treated realistically by supposing that the royal courts were the only real homes of law and that all other tribunals were the site of "alternative dispute resolution".

In today's world, when connections between English and Continental law are becoming closer, this historical treatment of England's past may be of broader than purely historical interest. The 'insularity' of English law has never been complete. It is a pleasure to welcome this English translation of a work that describes the connections.

R. H. Helmholz
Chicago, Illinois

Contents

Introduction

Perhaps I ought to commence by noting that in this book three specialized legal fields converge. First, obviously, canon law; but then also comparative law and legal history, notwithstanding the fact that the author is not a professional historian. Nor is the method followed strictly true to that discipline.

If I had to describe the approach used in this essay, I would say that it seeks to study a historical legal subject from the standpoint of comparative law. In this regard I am indebted to legal historians for their patient research labour. They unveil and arrange the historical data that other jurists can then use from the perspective of their own specialty.

The historical facts mentioned here are outlined only with the detail strictly necessary so that the reader does not to lose sight of the central argument to demonstrate how significantly canon law contributed to forming the Anglo-American legal tradition. However, I have tried to cite the relevant literature in every case.

As is explained later in this work, the greatest influence of the canon law occurred during the later Middle Ages. Therefore, the subject of investigation is essentially limited to an analysis of the impact that classical canon law had on the contemporary development of English law, which in turn constitutes the fundamental core of the broader, modern-day Anglo-American law.

In this context, we ought to bear in mind that the union between canon law and Roman law was then particularly close. Both legists and canonists gave life to the medieval *ius commune* which then dominated the legal world on the European continent. The foundations of continental law are as much of Roman as they are of canonical origin. And for that same reason, to speak of the influence of canon law on Anglo-American law is equivalent to speaking of the influence of the *utrumque ius*, a product of both ecclesiastical and civil sources. It must be said, however, that the ecclesiastical sources were primarily responsible for the inflow of continental legal notions into the British Isles during the Middle Ages. This explains why canon law is the focus of this study.

I recall that, while working on this project, a legal historian expressed his doubts about its viability. Perhaps, he said, it is premature: there are too many dark areas, much historical research still needs to be done on the subject. I then thought that, in some way, he was correct. But I also thought that, where history is concerned, it may always be too early to expound overall views on subjects as broad as this one. At some point it is useful to stop the clock and pause to elaborate a synthesis of the data unveiled to date by the historians, while at the same time seeking to provide the interpretation which may seem most rigorous — of course, without excluding that later research may correct conclusions once considered almost definitive or yield new elements offering changes in existing long established opinions.

On the other hand, it may seem surprising that someone not belonging to the Anglo-American tradition should address an issue that traditionally has been the realm of English, American, and Canadian authors (though none has approached it on a global basis). One might even be led to believe that despite being conversant in Anglo-American law, a propensity to overvalue the Roman and canonical contribution to common law systems might creep in. To counter this prejudice, should it exist, it is worth noting that the perspective of a civil lawyer can presumably be of use, precisely because it represents a point of contrast with the prevailing Anglo-American doctrine. In legal families or traditions what often happens in human families also occurs: some peculiarities are too evident and too customary to be seen from the inside — above all when they have not been noticed for a long time. They are more easily perceived from the outside and by foreigners.

The first version of this book was written in Spanish and published at the end of 1991. Considering the audience it sought to address, I thought it convenient to offer some explanations regarding certain general aspects of Anglo-American law which now might not be altogether necessary. Nevertheless, I have chosen to leave the original largely unaltered in this present English edition. I have only introduced an essential bibliographic update, which has in turn required some minor modifications to the text.

This work is the result of research conducted at the Universities of Cambridge (England) and Chicago, whose Law Faculties I had the honor of joining in a temporary and honorary capacity. In this regard, I want to express my gratitude to several persons.

Professor Richard H. Helmholz, of the University of Chicago, has been a constant source of aid and motivation, and has been kind enough to supervise meticulously and critically the typescript, making suggestions which contributed to improving it; our friendship has moved him to write a preface to this edition. Professor John H. Baker, of Cambridge University, apart from honoring me with his friendship and hospitality during the months spent in that city, took the time to guide me patiently through the study of English legal history which was indispensable to lay the foundations for the topic explored in this study. Professor Charles Donahue Jr. (Harvard University) put forward some useful observations in the initial phase of my work. A debt of the same kind, but even weightier, ties me to my friend Professor Stephan Kuttner (University of California-Berkeley) who honored me with a preface to the Spanish edition; and also to Professor Knut W. Nörr (University of Tübingen), whose kind help has enabled this English version to see the light of day.

Professor Rafael Navarro-Valls, of Complutense University (Madrid), with whom I have had the good fortune to work for quite a few years, also deserves separate mention. He gave me, some time ago, the initiative to investigate this subject. He was persuaded that it was extremely useful, not only for canon law, but also as a means of bridging the gap between the European and the Anglo-American academic environments, too often separated in the legal sphere. In the diverse stages of my work he has provided help in the way of thematic and bibliographic orientation; by substituting for me in my absence from Complutense University (where I was a Professor at that time); and by helping me to obtain the funding which made this project possible.

In this regard — the material aspect is important in research — I should also thank the Spanish Ministry of Education and the U.S.-Spanish Joint Committee for Cultural and Educational Cooperation for the grants that made my stays in Cambridge and Chicago possible.

Of decisive importance to this English edition has been the support provided by the Instituto de Investigaciones Jurídicas of the Universidad Nacional Autónoma of Mexico. Its director, my friend José Luis Soberanes, endowed with a historian and a comparatist's mind, immediately realized how useful and adequate the spread of this sort of work would be, and generously put at my disposal the funds and persons necessary for the costly and complex task of translation.

Finally, my friend Ignacio Foncillas, J.D. University of Chicago, aside from being one of the persons who contributed to making a unique experience of my stay in Chicago, has carefully revised and substantially improved the original translation

Part I

The Anglo-American Legal Tradition

Chapter 1

The Two Great Western Legal Traditions

1. Anglo-American Law and Continental Law

The eleventh century is perhaps the most important for the history of western law. In fact, in 1066, after winning the battle of Hastings William became, from being Duke of Normandy, William I, the Conqueror, King of England. With him the Anglo-American legal tradition, or common law[1], begins in a proper sense. Moreover, towards

[1] The term "legal tradition", used to refer to the great areas of legal culture that bind legal systems of common roots and characteristics, has been taken from J.H. Merryman, *The Civil Law Tradition. An Introduction to the Legal Systems of Western Europe and Latin America* (Stanford, 2d ed, 1985). There is an equivalent expression, "legal family", which is also frequent among comparative legal scholars (see, for example, R. David, *Les grands systèmes de droit contemporains* (Paris, 7th ed, 1978); and K. Zweigert / H. Kötz, *An Introduction to Comparative Law* (Oxford, 2d ed, 1987). At the same time, it should be clarified that the expression "common law" can have different meanings. It can be used to refer generically to the tradition of Anglo-American legal systems; and also to refer strictly to the law created by the English common law courts, as opposed to the law that was created by other royal courts (for instance equity, law merchant), or as opposed to what in the Continent is

the end of the same century, the first of the great western legal traditions — continental law — began a decisive phase in its development with the school of Bologna and the birth of a new generation of jurists who would promote the construction of the *ius commune* — the huge enterprise which would extend into the next centuries hand in hand with the rediscovery of Justinian Roman law and the elaboration of classical canon law.

Undoubtedly, these two legal traditions possess notable differences as a consequence of the diverse vicissitudes of their historical development. A Spanish scholar synthesized the situation acutely when he mentioned that, while continental law is based on norms, Anglo-American law is based on causes of action. Its evolution has been barely affected by the medieval conceptualization of Roman law[2].

It can be said that the continental tradition is rooted in Roman law, later to be shaped by the action of medieval Roman-canonical law, and, later still, by the stamp of legal absolutism, rationalism, and legal positivism. In short, its basic traits are the indubitable predominance of written law as a source of law — preferably codified in systematic bodies —, with the judiciary playing an essentially interpretive function, and a marked tendency towards conceptualization and theoretical constructs.

On the other hand, Anglo-American law was primarily formed of its own elements, alien to the Roman principles which are to be found at the core of European law. It grew gradually in an inorganic manner, marked primarily by judicial activity and political struggles between monarchy, nobility and bourgeoisie which shaped the course of the history of Great Britain. Because of this, it is characterized by profound customary roots, by judicial sources (it is a judge-made law), and by the preponderance of pragmatic solutions over logical constructions.

---

called "written law" (statutory law). The context usually makes it easy to understand the meaning of the expression in the particular case.

[2] See. A. de Cossío, "La concepción anglosajona del Derecho", *Revista de Derecho Privado* 233 (1947).

Certainly, it would be naive, and unreal, to ignore the profound differences that exist between these two methods of making and understanding law. To ascertain this, we need only observe — throughout history as in the present — aspects as basic as the diverse function that written legislation serves in each of those systems, the different understanding of the role of the judge, the value of judicial decisions, and even the methods of teaching law[3].

At the same time, it is true that from both perspectives — Anglo-American and continental — the differences between the two great legal traditions have often been exaggerated, and their common elements correspondingly minimized[4]. Habitually, continental as well as Anglo-American jurists have been more concerned with stressing the particularities and distinctive characters of their respective traditions, and have underestimated the extent to which they belong to the same

---

[3] It is interesting to note that the method of legal teaching had historically a crucial importance regarding the separation between the English and the continental law. In medieval Europe the jurists came from universities where Roman and canonical law were elaborated and propagated. In England instead they were trained around the common law courts, through the inns of court, and it was not a theoretical or academic teaching, but rather exclusively practical. For a comparative approach to both legal traditions, see the cited works of Cossío — from a continental perspective — and Merryman — from an Anglo-American point of view. See also G. Radbruch, *El espíritu del derecho inglés* (Madrid, 1958, Spanish version from the German original: *Der Geist des englischen Rechts*). For the current differences between the Anglo-American and continental areas regarding the teaching of law, see the suggestive observations of J.H. Merryman, "Legal Education There and Here: A Comparison", 27 *Stanford Law Review* 859 et seq. (1975).

[4] In the continental environment, one of the reasons is probably the attitude of our legal culture vis-à-vis the common law systems, which can be characterized by two words: ignorance and suggestion, insofar as common law holds the fascination of the unknown for many continental legal scholars (see. J.L. de los Mozos, "El sistema del *Common Law* desde la perspectiva jurídica española", in *Estudio de Derecho Civil en homenaje al Profesor J. Beltrán de Heredia y Castaño* (Salamanca, 1984), 541. It is probable that a similar observation can be made with respect to a significant part of Anglo-American legal scholars.

cultural and juridical world — the western legal tradition[5]. Thus they have not seldom largely ignored the fact that both traditions possess similar historical roots, which not only accounts for the frequent use of identical terminology and techniques, but also the sharing of an important nucleus of common concepts, principles and values[6].

In that respect, and insofar as the subject of this essay is concerned, the profound imprint left by both Roman and canon law on the civil law systems is usually acknowledged as an incontrovertible historical fact[7]. In contrast, however, that same imprint is too often reduced to a minimum where Anglo-American law is concerned, implying that it would be a peculiar phenomenon, hardly comprehensible for the systematic European mentality. Its growth would seem to have taken place in an almost absolute isolation from the legal doctrines elaborated on the Continent; as a consequence, English law would apparently have remained virtually cut off from Roman-canonical influence.

---

[5] See T.H. Bingham, "'There is a World Elsewhere': The Changing Perspectives of English Law", 41 *International and Comparative Law Quarterly* 513 et seq. (1992).

[6] See H.J. Berman, *Law and Revolution. The Formation of the Western Legal Tradition* (Cambridge, Massachusetts, 1983), 538 et seq.

[7] With regard to the influence of canon law on the continental legal institutions, see E. Bussi, *La formazione dei dogmi di diritto privato nel diritto comune* (Padova, 1937-1939, 2 vols.), and G. Le Bras, "Canon law", in C.G. Crump / E.F. Jacob, eds, *The Legacy of the Middle Ages* (Oxford, 1969, repr. of the ed of 1932), 321 et seq. See also the interesting synthesis elaborated in Spain by J. Maldonado, *La significación histórica del Derecho canónico* (Madrid, 1969). More specifically on procedural law, see A. Engelmann et al., *A History of Continental Civil Procedure* (Boston, 1927). From a broader perspective, referring to the influence of the Church on the western legal culture, see the suggestive and extensive monograph by H.J. Berman, *Law and Revolution. The Formation of the Western Legal Tradition*, already cited, and the two volumes by L. Lombardi Vallauri / G. Dilcher, eds, *Cristianesimo, secolarizzazione e diritto moderno* (Milano and Baden-Baden, 1981). For the influence of Christianity in Roman law, see B. Biondi, *Il diritto romano cristiano* (Milano, 1952-1954, 3 vols.).

It is precisely this supposed isolation which seems inadmissible in light of the most elemental historical evidence. At the time of William I's Conquest, England was an unequivocally Christian kingdom belonging within the same political and religious unity as the other medieval European kingdoms. It was virtually impossible that English law could remain impervious to the influence of that transnational legal system, canon law, which was being created to synthesize and spread the influence of the values contained in the Judæo-Christian heritage, and which has come to form part of the occidental cultural tradition, to which the common law clearly belongs[8].

For this reason Nörr has been able to say that within English law, together with the insular face represented by the customary common law, there also exists a European face, for which the Catholic Church is especially responsible. To the extent that England was a member of Christian Europe — affirms Nörr — it was shaped as much by the spiritual as by the temporal sphere: the first governed by canon law, and both controlled by the rules of medieval moral theology. Consequently, it is not surprising to find that ideas such as that of natural law — in its Thomistic sense —, equity or conscience, should infiltrate the secular sphere, and pervade its courts and its substantive law. The same can be said on occasions about specific rules — *canones et leges* — belonging to the *ius utrumque* constructed by continental jurists[9].

---

[8] See generally W.W. Bassett, "Canon Law and the Common Law", 29 *Hastings Law Journal* 1386 et seq. (1978). Among canonists, Stephan Kuttner had pointed out incidentally, thirty years ago, that research on the role played by canon law in the development of the common law was a very important task to be completed; the remark was made at the end of his well known speech pronounced in Rome in the official celebration of the 50th anniversary of the *Codex Iuris Canonici*, published under the title of S. Kuttner, "Il codice di Diritto Canonico nella storia", *Attività della Santa Sede* (Città del Vaticano, 1967), 1633 et seq. More recently, among Spanish scholars, the same point has been emphasized by R. Navarro-Valls, "La enseñanza universitaria del Derecho canónico en la jurisprudencia española", 1 *Anuario de Derecho Eclesiástico del Estado* 80-83 (1985).

It is important to note that this penetration does not imply that such influences are to be considered specifically foreign, or indeed alien to English law. Rather, "it was a matter of internal relations between different branches of the legal system in England, some of them being particularly English, some of them representing the European *ius commune* which had crossed the Channel"[10]. For the rest, exchange of legal influences between Continent and British Isles flowed in both directions, and one should not underestimate the repercussions that English legal constructions have had on the historical formation of continental law, on legal thinking as well as on the law-making process[11].

Well known is Holmes' opinion that knowledge of how continental law developed is necessary to fully comprehend the evolution of Anglo-American law[12]. In the same sense, and referring to certain attitudes of English historiography, Helen Cam stated categorically: "In our study of English medieval history, we are, perhaps, too ready to stay on our island. Considering the very close relations between England and Rome, and England and France during the greater part of the Middle Ages, our reluctance to look overseas and study parallel developments for enlightenment, is rather less than scientific"[13]. If, at the same time, we bear in mind that the medieval *ius utrumque* is the principal historical link between both legal traditions, the importance of analyzing the mark left by canon law on the configuration of the

---

[9] See K.W. Nörr, "The European Side of the English Law: A Few Comments from a Continental Historian", in *Englische und kontinentale Rechtsgeschichte: ein Forschungsprojekt* (Berlin, 1985), vol. 1, 15.

[10] Ibid.

[11] See ibid., 25 et seq.

[12] See. O.W. Holmes, *Collected Legal Papers* (New York, 1920), 301.

[13] H. Cam, "The Theory and Practice of Representation in Medieval England", in E.B. Fryde / E. Miller, eds., *Historical Studies of the English Parliament*, vol. 1 (Cambridge, 1970), 263.

common law — especially in the first centuries of its growth — is easily understood[14].

This analysis is what I will attempt to realize in the chapters of this essay. But even if only briefly, I should first of all set out some details of the history of English law and also formulate some questions regarding its relationships with the European legal environment.

2. Some Considerations on the Evolution of English Law

Of the invasions the British Isles have endured, the conquest led by William, Duke of Normandy, in 1066, was destined to be the one which most decisively affected the history of England[15]. More precisely, as far as the history of English law is concerned, it is with the Norman settlement that one can place the birth of the second — chronologically — of the western legal traditions: the common law. Of course the Conquest did not entail a start from nothing, but it resulted in the adoption of several measures which would end up by overcoming preexistent legal institutions — absorbing them at the same time — and would define the fundamental lines along which the evolution of its legal order was thereafter to flow.

It is not easy to synthesize the development of English law[16] in a systematic manner since its growth has occurred largely by judicial

---

[14] On the usefulness of this type of comparative studies, see the suggestive remarks of R. Zimmermann, *The Law of Obligations. Roman Foundations of the Civilian Tradition* (Cape Town & München, 1992), ix et seq.

[15] On the effects of the Norman Conquest upon the law of England, see generally G. Spence, *The Equitable Jurisdiction of the Court of Chancery* (Philadelphia, 1846), vol. 1, 87 et seq.

[16] Among the classic general treatises on the history of the common law, the following should be cited here: W.S. Holdsworth, *A History of English Law* (Boston, 4th ed., beginning in 1931); F. Pollock / F.W. Maitland, *The History of English Law before the Time of Edward I* (Cambridge, 2d ed., 1968); T.F.T. Plucknett, *A Concise History of the Common Law* (Boston, 5th ed., 1956). Among the more recent treatises, see J.H. Baker, *An Introduction to English Legal History* (London, 2d ed., 1979); S.F.C. Milsom, *Historical Foundations*

decisions. It has been inorganic, spontaneous; a growth resisting any attempt at rationalization according to the usual parameters of European doctrine. Holmes described this in a graphic manner when he asserted categorically that "the life of the law has not been logic, it has been experience". Or, as a French comparatist has written, Anglo-American law has been the result of perpetuating "the accidents of history"[17].

It is possible, however, to pinpoint the principal elements in that evolution. In this regard, it is probably Milsom who provides the key to understanding when he affirms that "the common law is the by-product of an administrative triumph, the way in which the government of England came to be centralized and specialized during the centuries after the Conquest"[18].

In effect, the objectives of the policy of the Norman and Angevin kings centered on achieving a strong, centralized government as a ductile instrument in the hands of the Crown. This policy included the creation of a solid machinery which would permit administration of justice in the name of the King — the doctrine of separation of powers was very far off.

One of the first measures undertaken by William the Conqueror to this end was splitting up the jurisdiction of ecclesiastical and royal courts. The following century and a half witnessed the final consolidation of the courts of common law around the expansion of a system of itinerant justice, and the creation of the two great central courts: the Court of King's Bench and the Court of Common Pleas, both taken from that large central administrative organism, the *Curia Regis*, stren-

---

of the Common Law (London, 2d ed., 1981). Also revealing is the reading of R.C. Van Caenegem, *The Birth of the English Common Law* (Cambridge, 1973), and J.H. Baker, introduction to the *Reports of Sir John Spelman*, vol. 2 (London: Selden Society, 1978).

[17] H.A. Schwarz-Liebermann von Wahlendorf, *Introduction à l'esprit et à l'histoire du Droit anglais* (Paris, 1977), 16-17.

[18] S.F.C. Milsom, *Historical Foundations*, 11.

gthened in the times of Henry II and established at the constitutional level by *Magna Carta*[19].

Gradually and inexorably, and mostly due to their efficiency, the royal courts displaced the local jurisdictions that existed before the Conquest[20]. They thus came to acquire a pre-eminence in the administration of justice in the kingdom, shared by the broad jurisdiction of the ecclesiastical courts (which maintained it up to some extent until well into the nineteenth century).

On the other hand, as the common law courts attained exclusivity in temporal jurisdiction, the limitations in their method of administering justice became manifest. This eventually led to the rise of other courts also dependent on the King, namely the Court of Chancery, the Court of the Star Chamber, and the Court of Admiralty[21]. They imparted justice according to different norms and criteria, and to some extent were in competition with the common law courts.

It would be beyond the scope of this study to detail the changes experienced by the English jurisdictional organization from the time of the Tudors until the great judicial reforms of the nineteenth century, which led to the changed system that is basically in force in the present day. However, it is interesting to mention briefly some of the charac-

---

[19] On the factors favoring the settlement of the royal jurisdiction, see F.W. Maitland, *The Constitutional History of England* (Cambridge, 1961; reprint of the 1st ed., 1908), 111-114. The reign of Henry II had a decisive significance for English law: his numerous legal reforms and initiatives constitute, to a large extent, the foundations on which the subsequent characteristic development of the common law were built. See in this respect J. Biancalana, "For Want of Justice: Legal Reforms of Henry II", 88 *Columbia Law Review* 433-536 (1988).

[20] The process, however, was not equally rapid in all areas of the law. Until the sixteenth century, some local courts (especially those of the boroughs and counties) retained competence and attributions of relative significance, although subject to some revision by the royal courts.

[21] To these we could add the Exchequer, which had jurisdiction over financial matters from ancient times, and was of a nature difficult to define. We could also mention the High Court of Chivalry, a court that had scarce significance in the history of English law.

teristics which have defined the common law from the beginning and marked its evolution in a decisive manner.

The first is its profoundly judicial character. It is a law which was born and grew, essentially, to the rhythm of the decisions of judges. On occasions, continental jurists describe the common law as a pure "consuetudinary" or "customary" law; this is rigorously inexact, unless we take custom (*consuetudo*) to mean the custom of the courts[22]. The common law is really compounded of judicial decisions, which declare what is law in each case, and which began to be remembered and recorded from an early date[23]. For this reason, describing instead the common law as "judge-made" law is more accurate.

The judicial activity of the common law courts was initially endowed with a certain flexibility, but acquired a progressive rigidity under the influence of two primary factors: the use of royal writs, and the link to precedent. This rigidity — as I will later explain — fulfilled an important function in the birth and development of the Chancery jurisdiction.

---

22 An Italian scholar has written, referring to English judges, that "their activity appeared then and appears now as an act of recognition of an already existent law, not as an act of will creating a new law. But, in fairness, English judges created, and still today create, new law when the circumstances of the particular case require it" (G. Pugliese, "Leyes, jueces, juristas, en la formación del Derecho romano y del *common law* inglés", *Anuario de Derecho Civil* 445 (1984).

23 The systematic collection of records is attributed to the reforms of the last years of Henry II's reign; see H. Brunner, "The Sources of English Law", in *Select Essays in Anglo-American Legal History*, vol. 2 (Boston, 1908), 29. In any event, it is worth clarifying that at the beginning of the common law judicial resolutions were far from constituting what is today understood as decisions — the judges did not formulate proper opinions, in the modern sense of the term. The ancient collections that describe what occurred in the English courts of justice are not comparable either with the current collections of decisions; the *Yearbooks* were rather private compilations of the pleadings that took place before the judges.

The writ, or form of action, was a document that entitled the royal courts to act, which has sometimes led the English procedure to be described as a formulary system. More precisely, the writ was an order emanating from the Chancery and directed to local authorities — especially the sheriff — indicating that in a certain case the proceedings were to be held before the royal courts[24]. Each writ was created for a specific set of facts, outside of which the court could not act. The plaintiff could not invent his own writ; he had either to find one which would prove appropriate to his circumstances or request the creation of a new one.

By the middle of the thirteenth century already there existed an abundant number of writs. Consequently the Provisions of Oxford, in 1258, prohibited the Chancery from elaborating new writs without the authorization of the King's Council, thus restraining the possible expansion of the common law. Later, the Statute of Westminster II

---

[24] The name of *writs* proceeds from the Latin term *breve*. They were one of the basic instruments utilized by the Crown in order to absorb the jurisdiction of the local courts. They were compiled in books with the title of "register of writs", which constitute an invaluable source for learning about the development of the common law during its initial centuries; see, in this regard, the introductions by E. Haas / G.D.G. Hall to their work *Early Registers of Writs* (London: Selden Society, 1970), especially vii et seq. and cviii et seq. It should be borne in mind, however, that the already mentioned notion of writs dates back to the times of Henry II, in the twelfth century. In their commencement, rather than orders aimed at the opening of a judicial process before the royal courts, the writs were instructions transmitted to the competent local authority (usually following a claim of the damaged party) compelling it to work in a certain manner in order to put remedy to an unjust situation which had come to the King's knowledge.

In relation to the concept and evolution of the system of writs, see generally R.C. Van Caenegem, *The Birth of the English Common Law*, 29 et seq., where the Dutch historian alludes to the existent analogies between writs and papal rescripts (Ibid., 59). A precise description of the beginnings of the common law procedure can be found in another book by Van Caenegem, *Royal writs in England from the Conquest to Glanvill* (London: Selden Society, 1959), 46 et seq.

(1285) gave the clerks power to devise new writs on the analogy of existing writs which did not quite fit the case — *in consimili casu* —, but this provision seems to have been little used. This hardening of the system was accelerated as the doctrine of *stare decisis* — to abide by previously decided cases — grew stronger in forensic practice, impelled by the progressive improvement of the recording of decisions.

In addition, we must consider the implantation of the jury from the time of Henry II, an institution which would promote the maturation of what, in the words of Coke, were "the entrails of the common law": the art of pleading developed by lawyers before the royal courts. Virtually everything in the common law system thus revolved around procedure. For this reason Baker has affirmed that, in English law, procedural institutions precede and cause substantive law[25]. Or, as Maine has written, "substantive law has at first the look of being gradually secreted in the interstices of procedure"[26].

In that same environment, at the inns of court[27], English jurists were being educated, attentive above all to the practical details of legal life,

---

25 See. J.H. Baker, *An Introduction to English Legal History*, 49.

26 Cited by F.W. Maitland, *The Forms of Action at Common Law* (Cambridge, 1954; reprint), 1.

27 The *inns of court* have their origin in the centralization of the administration of justice that took place in the first centuries of the common law. Initially they were created as places of lodging for lawyers, politicians, public servants and apprentices at law who made their way down to London when Parliament and the courts were in session. Especially apprentices found that lodging of great utility, insofar as it permitted them to learn the actual functioning of the law from practicing lawyers through more or less informal contacts. Though born as mere places of residence, they gradually became real associations of lawyers. Four of those inns reached a superior position by the late fourteenth century, and by the second decade of the fifteenth century almost all the judges and serjeants at law were elected from them. These four societies were called "inns of court" already by the Tudors' times, and even today constitute the center for the association of English lawyers. Their names are: Inner Temple, Middle Temple, Gray's Inn and Lincoln's Inn. On the inns of court, and generally on the evolution of the teaching of law in England, see J.H. Baker, *An introduction*, 132 et seq., and the bibliography there cited.

and unconcerned with the speculative questions into which their continental counterparts proceeding from universities — where legal teaching focused mainly on analysis of Roman and canon law — were initiated.

One can thus understand how, in this peculiar juridical climate, English law appeared destined to become largely impermeable to the theoretical constructs that, based on romanistic principles, were being developed by legists and canonists on the Continent. This isolation, in truth, did largely affect property law. In this respect, it should not be forgotten that another of the central characteristics of the common law is that it grew up in the midst of Europe's purest feudal society. A society where conflicts regarding property and possession of land were the ones which primarily attracted the response of the royal courts. It was land law of which the common law courts were particularly jealous, considering it their exclusive territory. For this reason, as I shall explain later, other legal areas in England were more accessible to the influence of continental doctrines.

Chapter 2

Isolation and European Inspiration on Anglo-American Law

1. The Presumed Insularity of English Law

Among classical English historians of law, it is frequent to find abundant references to the evolution of continental law, setting forth parallels with the development of the common law system or — when it was the case — noting the contrasts[1]. Nevertheless, more recent generations of British historians have usually adopted a very different and more "insular" perspective. In their scholarship, there is a inclination to minimize considerations of a comparative nature, because they presuppose that the evolution of continental law has had little influence in shaping the Anglo-American legal tradition. Consequently,

---

[1] See, in this regard, the works of Holdsworth, Plucknett, Pollock and Maitland, previously cited. There are another two well-known books on the subject: T.E. Scrutton, *The Influence of the Roman Law in the Law of England* (Cambridge, 1885), and W.W. Buckland / A.D. Mcnair, *Roman Law and the Common Law* (Cambridge, 1936; I have used a reprint of the 2d ed., Cambridge, 1965). It is also enlightening to read the writings of various authors which, under the title of *Select Essays in Anglo-American Legal History*, were edited in three volumes by the Association of American Law Schools, and published in Boston, between 1907 and 1909. On the Anglo-American historiography up to the sixties, there is an interesting essay written by a Spanish historian: J.A. Escudero Lopez, "La historiografía general del Derecho inglés", *Anuario de Historia del Derecho Español* 217-356 (1965).

these scholars tend to concentrate on the study of those internal factors which have contributed to development of the common law[2]. Contrariwise historians from the North American area have retained a more open attitude, and have, over the last two decades, conducted numerous studies along comparative lines, paying particular attention to the repercussion of classical canon law on the legal world of Great Britain[3].

In connection with these diverse attitudes towards the insularity of Anglo-American law, it is useful to bear in mind the observations made at the end of the prior chapter in regard to the peculiarities of the growth of the common law which endowed it with greater immunity from

---

[2] That way of thinking is followed, for example, by Baker and Milsom in their previously mentioned treatises. The insular approach, on the other hand, apparently proceeds from the opinions sustained by Maitland, who is undoubtedly the most influential author in the development of current English historiography. The most significant exceptions are likely Barton and Stein, due to their commitment to the study of Roman law; their works will be mentioned later on. A classical Italian comparatist has openly criticized the thesis of insularity maintained by Maitland, often uncritically accepted by continental jurists: see G. Gorla, "Diritto comparato", in *Cinquanta anni di esperienza giuridica in Italia* (Milano, 1981), 487 et seq. and 508 et seq.

[3] The principal focus for this line of North American legal historiography has been the Institute of Medieval Canon Law, promoted by Stephan Kuttner and located at the University of California (Berkeley) Law School for many years. Some of the more important names are Richard Helmholz, Norma Adams, Charles Donahue and Michael Sheehan; their writings will be referred to in due course. Much of the attention of these authors has centered on the study of English ecclesiastical case-law, considering — correctly — that the analysis of the history of Anglo-American law would remain incomplete without a comprehensive research on the highly significant jurisdiction exercised by the ecclesiastical courts in England during the Middle Ages (and, in some areas of law, until the nineteenth century). They have consequently accomplished extensive investigations into the records of the Church courts, often materialized as the publication of valuable documentation previously unpublished. See, for example, N. Adams / C. Donahue, Jr., *Select Cases from the Ecclesiastical Courts of the Province of Canterbury C.1200-1301* (London: Selden Society, 1981), and R.H. Helmholz, *Select Cases on Defamation to 1600* (London: Selden Society, 1985).

external influence. It is also useful to highlight — as a distinguished German historian has recently written — the fact that, in the search for the most noteworthy influences of medieval canon law in the British Isles, rather than on common law courts we ought to focus on other English courts — in particular the Court of Chancery and the Church courts[4].

Equally significant is the fact that, by the time the continental *ius commune* began to produce valuable innovations through the joint action of the legists and canonists of the classical era — the twelfth century —, royal legal procedure based on writs was sufficiently established in England. This meant that common law jurists did not need to resort to the new system coming from the universities as much as their continental counterparts[5]. Furthermore, according to Maitland's well-known thesis, the possibility of a massive reception of the romanistic legal culture was prevented in the sixteenth century by the strong resistance of the inns of court; this secured the continuity of the common law system, following a path staked out during the Middle Ages[6].

---

[4] See. K.W. Nörr, *The European Side of the English Law*, 18-19. Naturally, English courts were also influenced by the common law; see C. Donahue, Jr., "Ius commune, Canon Law, and Common Law in England", 66 *Tulane Law Review* 1773 et seq. (1992).

[5] See T.F.T. Plucknett, "The Relations between Roman Law and English Common Law down to the Sixteenth Century: A General Survey", 3 *University of Toronto Law Journal* 47 et seq. (1939). The same opinion, with particular reference to the reasons why the Roman-canonical procedure did not penetrate the practice of the common law courts, is sustained by R.C. Van Caenegem, "L'histoire du Droit et la chronologie. Réflexions sur la formation du *common law* et la procédure canonique", in *Études d'Histoire du Droit canonique, dediées à Gabriel Le Bras*, vol. 2 (Paris, 1965) 1459-1465.

[6] Maitland's thesis was explained in his famous Rede Lecture pronounced at Cambridge University and published in 1901 under the title of *English Law and the Renaissance*. An interesting commentary on it has been written by S.E. Thorne, "English Law and the Renaissance", in *La Storia del Diritto nel quadro delle scienze storiche* (Firenze, 1966) 437-445. Thorne maintains that the rejection of the reception of continental law was a consequence of more

All of the aforementioned elements naturally tend to support the insular perspective of English law. However, it is necessary to balance these against two elements of no lesser weight. The first is that the Anglo-American legal tradition was not shaped exclusively by the action of the common law courts. Alongside them, and with a broad jurisdiction, other courts imparted justice in England. Their jurisdiction may well be labeled complementary with that of the common law. In some cases it dated back to ancient times and lasted until the nineteenth century[7]. This was the case of the ecclesiastical courts, whose activity was based on canon law in its procedural as well as substantive aspects[8]. But there were also other courts which formed part of the royal legal system, and whose practice responded — at least to a certain degree — to the principles and norms of the civil law and canon law: namely, as mentioned before, the Courts of Chancery, the Star Chamber and the Admiralty[9].

---

complex causes than the mere resistance of the inns of court. A subsequent revision of Maitland's ideas has been made by J.H. Baker, introduction to *The Reports of Sir John Spelman*, vol. 2 (London: Selden Society, 1978) 24 et seq.; Baker is rather skeptical about the fact that the common law was then really threatened by a "massive" reception of civil law. However, a defence and re-interpretation of Maitland's theories has been performed by W.H. Dunham, bibliographical review, in 75 *Yale Law Journal* 1059 et seq. (1966); the review refers to the book of H.E. Bell, *Maitland: A Critical Examination and Assessment* (Cambridge, 1965).

[7] See C. Donahue, Jr., *Ius commune, Canon Law, and Common Law in England*, 1753 et seq., who also notes the decline experienced by these other courts, in favor of the common law courts, after 1640.

[8] In the following chapter I shall discuss the controversies regarding which canon law was applied by the English ecclesiastical courts.

[9] Actually, when the Probate, Divorce and Admiralty Division of the High Court was created in England in 1875, the only reason for that miscellany of jurisdictions seems to have been their common foundation on Roman and canon law rather than on common law; see G.L. Williams, *Learning the Law* (Cambridge, 11th ed., 1982) 5. The specific character of the Chancery jurisdiction was overtly recognized by the creation of the Chancery Division of the High Court.

The second factor weighing against the insularity of English law is more generic but, in my opinion, no less important. The English Kingdom belonged to the same cultural world as the rest of Europe. During the later Middle Ages — a critical time in the formation of the English legal system — England was indisputably a part of the community of Christian kingdoms. It was constantly involved in the complex struggles of the medieval political life — often playing a central role therein —, dominated by the unstable balance of tensions between the Papacy and the Empire, gradually paving the way for the modern state.

Above all, England was an active participant in the cultural currents circulating through the Continent. On both sides of the Channel the philosophical, theological, scientific, and artistic anxieties were essentially identical; unceasingly boiling, their backcloth was the Judæo-Christian heritage, and the universities were their principal stage (we should remember that Oxford is one the first European universities). It would seem very odd indeed if in the midst of this relatively uniform cultural environment, English law had remained locked away in a crystal tower, with a sterile growth free from infiltration by continental "germs"[10]. It would seem even more peculiar, when we take into account the constant flow of people between the two legal worlds in those centuries.

Consequently, it seems to me that the insularity view cannot be upheld in a radical manner. In addition to what I have said in the previous paragraphs — and without going into detail for the moment — some historical data suggests that English law was, from its beginning, in more or less close contact with continental legal developments[11].

---

[10] In regard to the diverse circumstances which converge on what has been called "legal transplant", see the suggestive remarks of C. Donahue, Jr., "What Causes Fundamental Legal Ideas? Marital Property in England and France in the Thirteenth Century", 78 *Michigan Law Review* 59 et seq. (1979).

[11] It is worth recalling that in Maitland's opinion — not particularly inclined to admit the continental influence, as we have seen — the term "common law" was taken from the expression "ius commune" utilized by the canonists. By the time of Edward I, it was already commonly used to designate the law applicable

One clear example is Lanfranc's presence in England — he was William's principal advisor in legislative matters. Lanfranc had taught law in Pavia and had later founded a school in Bec (Normandy), from which Anselm would later come to England and, as Archbishop of Canterbury, precipitate the investiture struggle. In the middle of the twelfth century, another Archbishop — Theobald — would bring Vacarius, who has been credited with opening the school of Roman and canon law in Oxford in 1149[12]. The Oxford school rapidly acquired fame and in a few years became a focus of attention towards the *ius civile* in England until Henry III, in 1234, prohibited the teaching of Roman law due to the imperialist connotations it had at the time[13].

The twelfth and thirteenth centuries would witness a considerable increase in interest in the canon law, beginning with the success of Gratian's *Decretum*[14]. It is therefore not surprising that the first two

---

to all Englishmen, as opposed to the written law, local custom and royal prerogative. At that moment it was not distinguished from "equity", since this name had not yet been applied to name a specific and separate body of rules. See F.W. Maitland, *Equity. A Course of Lectures* (Cambridge, 1949; reprint of the 2d ed) 2.

For the rest, I prefer not to refer here to the influence of canon law on the law of the Anglo-Saxon era. In this regard, see G. Spence, *Equitable Jurisdiction*, 9 et seq.; P.H. Winfield, *The Chief Sources of English Legal History* (Cambridge, Mass., 1925) 54 et seq. I shall not allude either to the significance of civil law and canon law for the legal evolution in Scotland. On this subject, see J.H. Baker, *An Introduction to English Legal History*, 31 et seq.; P. Stein, *The Character and Influence of the Roman Civil Law* (London, 1988), 319-360; R.C. Van Caenegem, *The Birth of the English Common Law*, 59 et seq.

[12] See F. De Zulueta / P. Stein, *The teaching of Roman law in England around 1200* (London : Selden Society, 1990).

[13] Calasso notes that the teaching of the *ius civile* could reinforce the subjection of the King to the Emperor; at the same time, English feudal lords feared that it could serve as a foundation for a monarchical absolutism contrary to their privileges. See F. Calasso, *Medio Evo del diritto* (Milano, 1954) 619.

[14] See W.W. Bassett, "Canon Law and the Common Law", 29 *Hastings Law Journal* 1395 et seq. (1978), and the bibliography cited therein. See also S.

treatises on common law — especially the second one — are influenced by their authors' focus on the "learned law" emerging from the Continent; these are the works ascribed to Ranulf Glanvill and Henry Bracton, written in the twelfth and thirteenth centuries respectively. To this, we should add the fact that among the first generations of common law judges there were a remarkable number of clerics conversant with canon law, and often with practical experience before the ecclesiastical courts[15]; this circumstance was necessarily significant, even though it had a greater effect on the administration of law than on its substance[16].

2. Anglo-American Law and Canon Law

In this light, we are entirely justified in seeking to explore further the relations between canon law and Anglo-American law, especially if we consider the magnitude of the task that medieval canonists decided to undertake from the initiation of the classical era with Gratian's *Decretum*[17].

Kuttner / E. Rathbone, "Anglo-Norman Canonists of the Twelfth Century", 7 *Traditio* 279 et seq. (1949-51), and the information on the existence of canon law books in English libraries provided by R.C. Van Caenegem, *Royal Writs in England from the Conquest to Glanvill* (London: Selden Society, 1959), 365 et seq.

[15] Maitland has written, referring to King Henry II, that "Henry's greatest, his most lasting triumph in the legal field was this, that he made the prelates of the Church his justices" (F. Pollock / F.W. Maitland, *The History of English Law*, 132).

[16] See P.H. Winfield, *Chief Sources of English Legal History*, 57-58.

[17] See the analysis of the interplay of the different political and legal forces in medieval Europe written by W. Ullmann, *Law and Politics in the Middle Ages* (Ithaca, N.Y., 1975). Particularly interesting are the chapters on the history of canon law and the history of its teaching (Ibid., 119-189). Also very suggestive is the explanation of the task of harmonization of sources and institutions that medieval canonists accomplished, provided by S. Kuttner, "Harmony from Dissonance: An Interpretation of Medieval Canon Law", within

That task indeed was an attempt to construct a complete legal system for the Catholic Church, based on Roman foundations from a technical standpoint, and based on scriptural, theological and philosophical foundations from the perspective of principle. At the same time, if we bear in mind the breadth and diversity of fields dominated by the medieval Church, it is not difficult to see that its law went far beyond what we today deem ecclesiastical matters. It encompassed an entire global legal system which reflected the Christian ideal of law[18]. Moreover, due to the characteristic religious and political unity of medieval Europe, that system was destined to acquire international dimensions, becoming the *ius commune* of Christendom, as a result of the combined work of canonists and civilians[19]. In fact it could even be said that, with classical canon law, the very notion of a legal system in a modern sense begins: i.e. a coherent group of norms and principles, based on a unitary government which possessed its own judicial mechanism, with a trained professional class of judges and lawyers, and conceived of as a system endowed with a logical unity. It was the object of scientific study, using the methods of scholasticism, similar to those contemporary philosophers and theologians were developing[20].

---

the author's collection of articles published under the title of *The History of Ideas and Doctrines of Canon Law in the Middle Ages* (London, 1980).

[18] A new and suggestive reinterpretation of the significance and main features of medieval canon law from Gratian has been recently written by R.H. Helmholz, *The Spirit of Classical Canon Law* (The University of Georgia Press, 1996).

[19] In relation to the elaboration of the *ius commune* and its influence on the legal and political life of Europe, I must refer again to the works of F. Calasso, *Medio Evo del diritto*, previously cited, and *Introduzione al diritto commune* (Milano 1970, reprint of the 1st ed.). The bibliography on this subject is immense, and there is no sense in providing here an exhaustive list. It is enough to mention a recent book which, moreover, contains plenty of bibliographical references: G. Santini, *Materiali per la storia del diritto comune in Europa* (Torino, 1990).

[20] See H.J. Berman, *Law and Revolution*, 85 et seq. and 143 et seq.

It is for these reasons that analysis of the relations between Anglo-American law and canon law cannot be confined to a detailed analysis of a series of specific norms or actions. Insofar as medieval canon law sought to embody and spread the Judæo-Christian legacy of values, its influence also came about via abstract legal principles. It is therefore necessary to focus on and analyze not only the precise rules of law and their practical application, but also the philosophy, moral theology and ecclesiology which inspired them[21].

On the other hand, study of these relations, as Helmholz has emphasized, opens analysis to three different perspectives: areas of cooperation between both legal systems, areas of conflict, and areas of possible reciprocal influence[22]. As examples of cooperation he mentions the willingness of the English Crown to incarcerate those excommunicated by the ecclesiastical jurisdiction[23], including excommunication of those who violated the provisions of the *Magna Carta*. The English nobles' rejection of the canonical doctrine regarding legitimization by subsequent marriage (the *nolumus leges Angliæ mutari* of the Statute of Merton, 1236), or the tensions arisen from the disputes over the jurisdiction of cases relating to breach of faith[24], are good examples of situations of conflict.

---

[21] Berman notes that "in the twelfth century the canonists and Romanists of western Europe combined the Greek capacity for philosophy with the Roman capacity for law. In addition, they deepened the earlier concepts of reason and equity by adding to them the Judaic and Christian concept of conscience" (ibid.,146).

[22] See R.H. Helmholz, "Canon Law and English Common Law", in his collection of articles published under the title of *Canon Law and the Law of England* (London, 1987), 2.

[23] See F.D. Logan, *Excommunication and the Secular Arm in Medieval England* (Toronto, 1968); E. Vodola, *Excommunication in the Middle Ages* (Berkeley and Los Angeles, 1986), 164 et seq.; R.H. Helmholz, *The Spirit of Classical Canon Law*, 358 et seq.

[24] See R.H. Helmholz, *Canon Law and English Common Law*, 3 et seq.; W.R. Jones, "The Two Laws in England: The Later Middle Ages," 11 *Journal of Church and State* 111-131 (1969), and, of the same author, "Relations of the

It is, however, the third perspective which has been chosen for this work. But, before proceeding, I ought to clarify certain details which are relevant to the study undertaken in the following chapters.

First, we should not lose sight of the fact that in the research of this subject, it is not always easy or even possible to distinguish between canon law and medieval Roman law. Both emerged from the same university environment, and both were often cultivated by the same people, as a logical consequence of the spiritual unity of medieval Europe, in which ethical and political differences appeared to dissolve[25]. As Calasso has indicated, the great forces which gave life to that unity were the Latin culture, which impregnated every corner of Europe, and the Christian faith that transformed it; the effort to separate what was properly Roman and what was of Christian origin would be vain, since Latin culture was unthinkable without the Christian faith and vice versa[26].

That union between Roman and Christian elements is the reason why canon law not only contributed specifically Christian contents to English law, but also became the main conduit through which Roman law entered the British Isles during the Middle Ages[27]. Hence Winfield could write that we should focus on canon law, rather than just on the *ius civile*, to discover the most decisive influence of Roman law on the Anglo-American legal tradition[28].

Two Jurisdictions: Conflict and Cooperation during the Thirteenth and Fourteenth Centuries", in W.M. Bowsky, ed, *Studies in Medieval and Renaissance History*, vol. 7 (Lincoln, Nebraska, 1970), 77-210.

[25] On the influence of Roman law on canon law, in substantive as well as in procedural aspects, see S. Kuttner, "Some Considerations on the Role of Secular Law and Institutions in the History of Canon Law", in *Scritti di sociologia e politica in onore di Luigi Sturzo*, vol. 2 (Bologna, 1953), 349 et seq.

[26] See F. Calasso, *Medio Evo del diritto*, 326.

[27] See H.D. Hazeltine, "Roman and Canon law in the Middle Ages", chapter 21 of *The Cambridge Medieval History* (Cambridge, 1926), 758 et seq.

[28] See P.H. Winfield, *Chief Sources,* 55. On the other hand, some authors have emphasized the superiority of canon law over medieval Roman law, due to

On the other hand, I think one should avoid the obsession of just singling out the different elements in the Anglo-American legal system that have unequivocal and clear canonical roots. All that we would obtain would be a collection of loose parts lacking significance as a whole. Certainly, through time, a legal system gradually builds itself from diverse elements that, at a given moment, have clearly recognizable origins. But, as the system takes fuller shape, these elements acquire a new and different reality once they are integrated into the totality. Thus the task of dissecting the living legal body in order to observe each member in its original purity — now non-existent — inevitably fails and distorts the reality.

If I may use an analogy, I would say that in law something similar to what occurs in painting a picture takes place. While the picture is being painted each brush stroke has a definite form and colour. But, as brush strokes intermingle, forms and colours fade, and the original existence of each brush stroke withers away, becoming part of a new, much more perfect, reality. What is then important is not each one of the artist's separate movements, but the finished painting itself, even though it is known — and the studious may well wish to know — how it has been achieved.

It should also be pointed out that, frequently, reception of the canon law in England was not linear. Rather, English jurists took their inspiration from canonical solutions or principles in order to create their own solutions — sometimes their sources being rapidly forgotten — and adapted them to the particular necessities and circumstances of their own legal environment.

For that reason, my fundamental goal will be to discover the presence of canonical creations in the evolution of the English legal world, not so much to show their survival in the details (what really exists is *living*, existent law), as to assess the extent to which canon law

---

its greater attention to the particular circumstances of cases and persons, derived from the Christian concept of human person; see C. Lefevbre, "Equity in Canon Law", in R.A. Newman, ed, *Equity in the World's Legal Systems. A Comparative Study Dedicated to René Cassin* (Brussels, 1973) 93.

has taken a part in the configuration of Anglo-American legal institutions.

Canonical contributions sometimes took place through the great principles of law. One example is provided by Plucknett, when he points out the role played by religion in the formation of the medieval idea of law: a law which is considered divine in its origin, supreme in its authority, rendering justly to every man his due [29]. Another example is recalled by Strayer, when he refers to the Church's insistence that imparting justice is one of the essential attributes of secular power, thus aiding materially to reinforce the system of royal jurisdiction[30].

At other times, however, the influence of canon law has occurred through contact with specific legal norms or judicial solutions. In either case, it will frequently be necessary to resort to conjectures or probabilities, given the practical difficulties of proving with absolute certainty any causal connection between contemporary historic events. In such situations, however, I personally feel inclined to presume the influence of canon law wherever the mere *possibility* (though not the *certainty*) of that influence exists, since I believe that law does not normally arise by spontaneous generation, and that it is more likely that a jurist will incorporate elements from an alien system which he knows, than create his own solutions *ex novo* ignoring an experience which is both nearby and effective[31].

In connection to this, Helmholz has mentioned two objections that could be made against the effective influence of canon law on common law[32].

---

[29] T.F.T. Plucknett, *Concise History*, 40.

[30] J.R. Strayer, *On the Medieval Origins of the Modern State* (Princeton, 1970), 31-32.

[31] In a similar sense, C. Donahue, Jr., *Ius commune, Canon Law, and Common Law in England,* 1748, has written that, though it is not always possible to unequivocally demonstrate conscious borrowings, it is possible to speak "of parallels, of similarities of language, of coincidences that seem too striking to be coincidental".

[32] See R.H. Helmholz, *Canon Law and English Common Law*, 15 et seq.

First, a supposed ignorance of canon law by common lawyers. In this regard, it should be pointed out that, even though we cannot presuppose that they had a detailed knowledge of canon law, neither would it be exact to presume their absolute ignorance of it. On the contrary, common law jurists had a certain familiarity with so-called "learned laws", especially through the *regulæ iuris* included in various Roman and canonical texts in common use within the British Isles. Moreover, canon law was then a highly operative law in England, taking jurisdiction over many aspects of life that are today reserved for secular law; it is unrealistic to suppose that English judges and lawyers were completely unaware of the solutions contributed by a jurisdiction which was a continual source of legal practice within the kingdom, side by side with the royal courts[33].

The second objection would be based on the attitude of English jurists, allegedly reticent in admitting foreign ideas. Against it, we should bear in mind that the kind of influence addressed here does not entail adopting a completely alien legal system. Rather, it is a question of showing how English jurists adopted — and adapted — ideas taken from canon law just as they did with ideas taken from other legal systems. Incorporation and adaptation of solutions from outside did not make them lose control over their own system, since they selected and modified the exterior sources of law. We should note in addition that canon law was not in fact a completely alien law for the common lawyers. It is true that it was mostly elaborated on the Continent, but it is also true that certain sectors of English legal life — family law was an example — were under the ecclesiastical jurisdiction. Therefore, though not being royal law, canon law was very much a part of the English legal system.

To draw together the first part of this study I should explain the organization of the contents of the two remaining parts. I have devoted the second part to exploring the points of connection between canon law and English law that made canonical influence possible. In the third

---

[33] This fact, on the other hand, is confirmed by the existence of conflicts between both jurisdictions, to which I will refer in the following chapter.

part, I proceed to describe the specific canonical contributions to the various areas of law.

Part II

The Routes of Entry of Canon Law into England

When we attempt to analyze the influence of one legal order on another, it is obviously not sufficient to identify existing parallels among them and then attribute the "influencing" to that legal order which arrived at or adopted a particular position first in time. Rather, it is necessary to locate the points of contact between the two legal worlds — the causal nexus, or at least the reason that can explain the supposed influence.

This is why, in investigating this subject, the first task is to detect the channels by which canon law managed to penetrate and affect the legal life of England. Historically, it is not difficult to identify the three main routes of entry: the courts of the Church, the Court of Chancery, and jurisprudence or legal doctrine.

It may be noticed that I have made no mention of another English court which has been traditionally linked to continental law, namely the Court of Admiralty, born in the middle of the fourteenth century and empowered with jurisdiction over matters of mercantile and maritime law[1].

---

[1] Its importance notably declined from the seventeenth century, for its jurisdiction ended up being absorbed by the common law courts, which were jealous of the competence possessed by the Court of Admiralty and strongly opposed to its inclination towards the *ius civile*. About the history of the Court of Admiralty and the rest of the courts mentioned here, see the general

Certainly, the Court of Admiralty received and applied continental legal practice and doctrine, in procedural as well as substantive aspects. However, especially with regard to the latter, the influence was exerted by principles of Italian civil law rather than canon law[2]. Furthermore, as the British empire gained control of the seas in modern times, and as common law courts gradually usurped the competence of the Court of Admiralty, this field of English law itself became much more insular, abandoning the internationalist perspective that had characterized its origins.

---

treatises cited in note 16 of chapter 1. Moreover, in relation to the ecclesiastical courts in England, see J.L. Barton, "Roman Law in England", in *Ius Romanum Medii Ævi*, pars V, 13th (Milano, 1971) 79 et seq. In relation to the Court of Admiralty and its struggle with the common law, see the monograph by D.R. Coquillette, *The Civilian Writers of Doctor's Commons, London* (Berlin, 1988) 97 et seq.

[2] The specific degree of that influence has not been studied in detail yet. In any event, referring specifically to the procedural aspects of the Court of Admiralty, it does appear that there was a significant influence of the Roman-canonical procedure, similar to influence received by other English courts with special jurisdiction, namely the Court of Request, the High Court of Chivalry or the Court of the Star Chamber . Yet these courts disappeared or lost importance since the seventeenth century, in favor of the common law courts. See C. Donahue, Jr., "Ius Commune, Canon Law and Common Law in England", 66 *Tulane Law Review* 1753 et seq. (1992).

Chapter 3

Ecclesiastical Courts

It is not necessary to remark once again upon the widespread dominance the Church exerted over almost every aspect of life in Europe during the Middle Ages. This dominance existed not only in the religious sphere, but also in the political, scientific, and artistic fields. In a way and with an intensity strongly contrasting with today's mentality, the lives of people, kingdoms, and institutions, were inevitably affected by ecclesiastical presence and intervention. In the legal domain, that influence was primarily exerted through application of canon law, which gained momentum first with the revitalization of the Roman pontificate from the time of the Gregorian reformation (late eleventh century), and then with the unprecedented improvement that canon law itself experienced from the time of Gratian's *Decretum* (mid twelfth century).

On the other hand, the influence of canon law on western law came about not only through its merger with Roman law into what has been termed the *ius commune* of medieval Europe. Canon law also contributed to the shaping of diverse legal institutions in Europe by virtue of the broad jurisdiction exercised by ecclesiastical courts. That action proved especially profound and long-lasting in certain specific areas of law (archetypally the law of marriage[1]).

---

[1] On this specific subject one of the best works ever written is that of A. Esmein, *Le mariage en Droit canonique* (Paris, 1929), 1-66.

England was not an exception to that phenomenon, as it is confirmed by the jurisdiction exercised by the Church courts, and by their relations with royal jurisdiction.

1. The Jurisdiction of the "Court Christian"

In the English kingdom, ecclesiastical courts enjoyed a jurisdiction which in certain ways was even broader than that exercised on the Continent. The jurisdictional power of the Church was foreshadowed before the Norman invasion, though with rather diffuse boundaries: in the local Anglo-Saxon system of justice, it was common for clergymen and important laymen to sit together in the same tribunals to judge both spiritual and temporal matters[2].

Only in the years immediately following the Conquest does the jurisdictional situation start to become clearer. In Plucknett's opinion, the attitude of William I towards the Church was to strengthen it internally while at the same time limiting its political power[3]. This is

---

[2] I have already stated that I have preferred to omit an analysis of the legal situation in England during Anglo-Saxon times, since the starting point of the Anglo-American legal tradition is actually the Norman Conquest, in 1066. Nevertheless, it is worth recalling that there was an intense mutual influence between pre-classical canon law and the laws of Germanic origin, in the British Isles as in the rest of Europe. An interesting historical example of that influence, during the early Middle Ages, are the so-called "penitential books" or *libri pœnitentiales*: catalogues of moral offences with their corresponding sanctions, which became enormously widespread in Great Britain and in Ireland. See T.P. Oakley, *English Penitential Discipline and Anglo-Saxon Law in their Joint Influence* (New York, 1969; reprint of the 1923 ed). Generally on Anglo-Saxon England, see H.R. Loyn, *Anglo-Saxon England and the Norman Conquest* (New York, 1962).

[3] T.F.T. Plucknett, *Concise History*, 12. William the Conqueror's attitude did not imply that he recognized the independence of the Church; contrariwise, his purpose was to control ecclesiastical power and subject it to his governmental interests. Actually he substituted all the bishops in England, except two, for prelates of Norman origin, and did not hesitate to occasionally enact laws on ecclesiastical matters, binding for the Church in England as

why, shortly after assuming power, he decided to separate the jurisdictions of ecclesiastical and civil courts — a step described by Stubbs as "the most important ecclesiastical measure of the reign"[4]. That separation led to a progressive differentiation between the organization of the two jurisdictions, the spiritual and the secular. By the middle of the thirteenth century, the Church had already established a complete network of courts in place with a hierarchical structure ascending from the local jurisdiction to the Holy See[5].

However, this separation of jurisdictions was not rigid at the outset[6]. It is only from the thirteenth century that the jurisdictional boundaries would gradually be settled by means of "writs of prohibition" — orders directed by the royal jurisdiction to

---

well as in Normandy (see H.J. Berman, *Law and Revolution*, 435 et seq.). Furthermore, in a decree of 1067 William declared that the King of England and Duke of Normandy possessed the power to determine whether a particular Pope should be recognized by the Church within his territories, established that no ecclesiastical council in his kingdom could dictate canonical norms without his consent, and provided that the King had the power to veto ecclesiastical punishments imposed on his nobles. The text of the decree can be seen in W. Stubbs, *Select Charters and Other Illustrations of English Constitutional History from the Earliest Times to the Reign of Edward I* (Oxford, 1913), 95-99.

[4] W. Stubbs, *The Constitutional History of England, in its Origin and Development*, vol. 1 (Oxford, 3rd ed, 1880), 283.

[5] With regard to the reach of the measure adopted by William I, see C. Morris, "William and the Church Courts", 82 *The English Historical Review* 449-463 (1967). Morris maintains that William I's ordinance — between 1072 and 1076 — was certainly the starting point for the separation of jurisdictions, but a complete system of ecclesiastical courts, with its own procedure and personnel, and with a relatively well defined area of competences, was gradually created throughout the twelfth century.

[6] See W.R. Jones, *The Two Laws in England*, 116 et seq.

ecclesiastical courts requiring that they abstain from giving judgment in cases considered reserved for the common law[7].

In canonical theory, exclusive competence over spiritual matters and cases in which clergymen were involved belonged to ecclesiastical jurisdiction, but in fact it seems that the Church of England exercised virtually no jurisdiction whatsoever over clergymen in civil causes[8]. On the other hand, in criminal law it was not always easy to elucidate to which one of the two jurisdictions prosecution of a clergyman belonged (this fact would cause the confrontation between Henry II and Thomas Becket regarding what, in canon law, was known as the *privilegium fori* or "benefit of clergy": i. e. the ecclesiastical jurisdiction's privilege to exclusive jurisdictional competence over offenses committed by the clergy). In addition, there was the difficulty of determining which matters were properly considered "spiritual"; the Church had a marked tendency to extend the meaning of that term, in contrast to the more restrictive view held by the Crown[9].

---

[7] See W.W. Bassett, *Canon Law and the Common Law*, 1407 et seq.; G.B. Flahiff, "The Writ of Prohibition to Court Christian in the Thirteenth Century", 6 *Medieval Studies* 261 et. seq. (1944), and 7 *Medieval Studies* 229 et seq. (1945); R.H. Helmholz, "The Writ of Prohibition to Court Christian before 1500", 43 *Medieval Studies* 297 et seq. (1981). It has rightly been pointed out that the writs of prohibition were "indirect in the sense that they required application by one of the parties to litigation in the ecclesiastical forum", but "prohibitions were direct and forceful in the sense that they proclaimed that the English Crown, and not the canon law, was the ultimate arbiter of the Church's jurisdictional competence": R.H. Helmholz, *Roman Canon Law in Reformation England* (Cambridge, 1990), 22.

[8] See R.H. Helmholz, *Roman Canon Law in Reformation England*, 9 et seq.

[9] On the other hand, Richardson and Sayles mention some twelfth century cases which show that the royal courts — formed by nobles as much as by prelates — continued to exercise actual jurisdiction on ecclesiastical matters. H.G. Richardson / G.O. Sayles, *The Governance of Medieval England from the Conquest to Magna Carta* (Edinburgh, 1963), 285 et seq.

Reality, therefore, was a great deal more complex than one would have concluded simply from the political measures of separation adopted by William the Conqueror. And it is beyond doubt that many aspects in the life of an ordinary citizen were subject to the exclusive jurisdiction of the Church courts. As Maitland has written: "Every layman, unless he were a Jew, was subject to ecclesiastical law. It regulated many affairs of his life, marriages, divorces, testaments, intestate succession; it would try to punish him for various offences, for adultery, fornication, defamation; it would constrain him to pay tithes and other similar dues; in the last resort it could excommunicate him and then the state would come to its aid"[10].

To be more precise, in the later Middle Ages the ecclesiastical courts exercised jurisdiction, first, over matters directly related to the organization of the Church. This was the case with determination of the clerical status of a person, and the judgment of criminal causes involving clergymen. They even came to exercise jurisdiction over disputes over ownership of land — the clearest area theoretically reserved for the common law — when the land had been given in free alms to the Church.

The field in which ecclesiastical courts exercised the most undisputed jurisdiction was probably marriage. Not only did they decide questions involving the validity, nullity, separation and dissolution of the bond, but also issues connected with it, such as the legitimacy of children[11], or diverse aspects of marital property,

---

[10] F. Pollock / F.W. Maitland, *History of English law*, vol. 1, 439.

[11] On this matter, however, ecclesiastical jurisdiction lost an important struggle against the common law, when the English nobility unanimously rejected the canonical doctrine according to which offspring became legitimized by subsequent marriage (Statute of Merton, 1236, c. 9: "nolumus leges Angliæ mutari", we do not want the laws of England to be changed). Here we can observe the zeal of the common law courts in trying to preserve the land law as its own exclusive territory, for the issue of legitimacy of children did not involve just a moral question; the actual relevant question was the right to inherit the land, which in principle could not be granted in testament, but was passed onto the heir in accordance with the typically

especially when the ownership of land was not in dispute. That jurisdiction would be prolonged essentially until 1857, when it would be transferred to a new "Court for Divorce and Matrimonial Causes".

Ecclesiastical jurisdiction over probate extended for the same period — i.e. the validity and interpretation of wills, administration of legacies, and intestacy. This jurisdiction had two momentous side effects on the common law. One is the rise of the executor as the central figure in the English law of succession. The other is the crucial importance of the distinction between personal and real property, since inheritance of property by testament was possible only for personal property, while testators were not, as a rule, free to dispose of their land. Common law courts tended to center their attention on problems relating to real property — inheritable only by those whom customary feudal rules designated — and ecclesiastical courts limited their jurisdiction to inheritance of personal property[12].

The Church also exercised practically undisputed jurisdiction in tithes — a matter of no negligible importance in those times. Likewise, criminal law — which in theory belonged to the courts of the Crown — also suffered the "intrusion" of ecclesiastical jurisdiction, under the banner of seeking the expiation of sin and procuring the health of the sinner's soul. Thus Church Courts exercised a wide jurisdiction not only in cases related to violence against clergymen, but also expanded their competence into repression of defamation, usury, simony, perjury, witchcraft, and sexual offences — adultery, fornication and incest.

In the field of contract, the ecclesiastical courts grounded their claims on their jurisdiction over perjury. They exercised a significant jurisdiction directed to protect the wronged party in cases of non-performance of a sworn promise. The cases centered on the issue of

---

feudal rules of medieval England. The position of English law would continue to be the same until the Legitimacy Act of 1926.

[12] See W.S. Holdsworth, *History of English Law*, vol. 1, 128.

fidei læsio or "breach of faith"[13] — the plaintiff argued that the breaching party had pledged his Christian faith upon promising to perform contractual obligation ("pledge of faith"), and this justified the intervention of Church courts.

Even in the domain of real property there was some intervention by the ecclesiastical power: in the execution of uses, before the Chancery jurisdiction absorbed those causes[14].

2. Conflicts and Cooperation between Ecclesiastical and Royal Jurisdiction

In view of the active role played by the ecclesiastical courts during the later Middle Ages and their quest to expand their jurisdiction, it would be naive to suppose that such efforts would not have met with opposition by the common law courts[15]. Indeed, historical evidence indicates that rivalry between both jurisdictions grew as the common law underwent a process of technical improvement, growing increasingly jealous of ecclesiastical interference[16].

Relations were not exclusively conflictive, however. There were areas of cooperation between secular and spiritual power. I have

---

[13] This occurred to such a degree that, by the middle of the fifteenth century, this sort of litigation had come to dominate the business of most ecclesiastical courts in England. See R.H. Helmholz, *Roman Canon Law in Reformation England*, 25; B. Woodcock, *Medieval Ecclesiastical Courts in the Diocese of Canterbury* (London, 1952), 89 et seq.; R.M. Wunderli, *London Church Courts and Society on the Eve of the Reformation* (Cambridge, Mass., 1981), 104 et seq.

[14] See R.H. Helmholz, "The Early Enforcement of Uses", 79 *Columbia Law Review* 1503 et seq. (1979).

[15] A succinct and suggestive description of the ecclesiastical courts' effective domain in that time, and of their conflicts with the common law courts, can be read in R.H. Helmholz, *Roman Canon Law in Reformation England*, 1 et seq.

[16] See P.H. Winfield, *Chief Sources*, 58.

already mentioned the Crown's willingness to imprison the people who had been excommunicated by the Church, and also the excommunication which could be imposed on persons who violated the provisions of the *Magna Carta*. Moreover, Bassett has pointed out that during the thirteenth and fourteenth centuries the Crown permitted, and even promoted, litigation in ecclesiastical courts and appeals to Rome, so long as this was not to the detriment of the King's rights[17].

This cooperation has led some scholars to argue against exaggerating the struggles between the two jurisdictions — attributable to the fact that canon law and common law were both in development at that time — and to underline instead the importance of areas of collaboration. As Jones has written, "jurisdictional conflict in England was limited, specific, and pragmatic — a steady but gentle pressure by the King's courts on those of the Church"[18]. On the other hand, collaboration was possible, among other reasons, because of the frequent contacts between jurists from those two branches of English law, which provided the opportunity for mutual influence[19].

In any event, for our purposes it is not necessary to put conflict and cooperation on the balance in order to determine which was more prominent. What it is needed is to highlight two factors relevant to our study.

First, on numerous occasions royal courts took over jurisdiction in areas where their ecclesiastical counterparts had been active, or where religious jurisdiction had seemed to emerge naturally. Two clear examples may be mentioned in this regard. One is the executor, a figure which, having been created by the ecclesiastical courts,

---

[17] See W.W. Bassett, *Canon Law and the Common Law*, 1409.

[18] W.R. Jones, *Relations of the Two Jurisdictions*, 204. See also his other work cited here, *The Two Laws in England*, 111 et seq.

[19] See C. Donahue, Jr., *"Ius Commune", Canon Law, and Common Law*, 1762 et seq.

gradually fell under the control of common law courts[20]. The other, with lesser long term effects for English law, is the jurisdiction exercised by Chancery over witchcraft during certain periods in the fifteenth century[21].

Second, for a long time, despite the aforementioned and despite regular use of writs of prohibition, canon law courts exercised jurisdiction over matters which the common law sought to claim exclusively. So it happened, for example, in certain matters related to tithes, or in some cases concerning debts[22], as where a "breach of faith" was alleged (breach of the faith pledged in the contract)[23]. It ought to be noted that such an expansionist attitude of the ecclesiastical courts was not the product of an unconstrained zeal for unduly extending their own jurisdiction. Rather it often rested on an apparent unwillingness by the royal courts to take active steps fully to enforce long-standing principles of the English common law[24].

On the other hand, effective restriction of the Church's medieval jurisdiction occurred, not through writs of prohibition, but through frequent use of actions based on the fourteenth century statute of *Præmunire*. The statute had originally been meant to prevent appeals to the Roman court, but, under an expanded interpretation — beginning in the 1480's — it was read to apply also to litigation in the spiritual courts within England itself. In short, that interpretation

---

[20] See R. Caillemer, "The Executor in England and on the Continent", in *Select Essays in Anglo-American Legal History*, vol. 3, ,746-769; M.M. Sheehan, *The Will in Medieval England* (Toronto, 1963), 148 et seq.

[21] See W. Barbour, "Some Aspects of Fifteenth Century Chancery" , 31 *Harvard Law Review* 853 et seq. (1918).

[22] Obligations derived from breach of contract, relating to a sum of money or a determined quantity of fungible goods.

[23] See W.R. Jones, *Relations of the Two Jurisdictions*,165 et seq.; R.H. Helmholz, *Canon Law and the Law of England*, 3 et seq. and 59 et seq. Helmholz affirms that "the writ of prohibition was not decisive in determining the actual scope of ecclesiastical jurisdiction" (Ibid., 60).

[24] See R.H. Helmholz, *Roman Canon Law in Reformation England*, 25.

presupposed that, in some matters, the people sued before an ecclesiastical court could prevent the process by alleging that the proceedings in the ecclesiastical forum were being taken in derogation of the rights and dignity of the English Crown. An additional consequence of invoking the statute was that the plaintiff was often subjected to the payment of damages as well as to the criminal penalties laid out in the statute. The natural result was that, in light of the risks entailed in bringing a lawsuit before ecclesiastical courts — particularly concerning testamentary debt, breach of faith and defamation involving the imputation of temporal crimes — potential plaintiffs began to redirect their actions to other jurisdictions[25].

3. The Law Applied by English Ecclesiastical Courts

From our discussion heretofore, the decisive role played by ecclesiastical courts in England seems unquestionable. However, before concluding this chapter, it is still necessary to examine what substantive law was applied, and this in turn raises two additional questions.

The first one refers to the possible changes caused by Henry VIII's separation from the Roman Church. The response is rather straightforward, and unanimously shared by scholars who have studied the subject. As Holdsworth has noted, following the Act of Supremacy the King replaced the Pope as the source of ultimate judicial authority in the Church courts; yet the canon law applied in them remained fundamentally unchanged[26], at least as long as it did not clash with the King's legislation[27].

---

[25] See ibid., 25 et seq.

[26] See W.S. Holdsworth, *History of English Law*, vol. 1, 593; and, more recently, the analysis of the jurisdiction exercised by ecclesiastical courts over matrimonial and sexual matters, made by M. Ingram, *Church Courts, Sex and Marriage in England, 1570-1640* (Cambridge, 1990; reprint of the 1st ed, 1987), 41 et seq.

[27] J.H. Baker, introduction to *The Reports of Sir John Spelman*, 70.

Furthermore, this continuity was not limited to the substantive law applied, but also to the scope of the jurisdiction exercised by the ecclesiastical courts. Indeed, the Reformation was so careful of any rupture with the preexisting order that Helmholz, after an accurate study of the matter, has affirmed that, compared to the changes occurring after the accession of the Tudors, ecclesiastical jurisdiction actually underwent fewer alterations in the years going from the start of the "official" Henrician Reformation in 1529 until 1570: in the main, the Church's position was left intact by the Reformation statutes[28].

Of course, as time elapsed the Reformation would leave a considerable imprint in certain areas[29]. However, we ought not overestimate that influence[30]. The continuity of medieval tradition extended even to procedural norms, which were hardly influenced by the common law since the judges and lawyers who practiced in the

---

[28] See R.H. Helmholz, *Roman Canon Law in Reformation England,* 28-54 and 158-162.

[29] A detailed analysis of the changes that took place in specific areas of the post-Reformation courts practice can be seen in ibid., 55-120.

[30] For example, in marriage law, despite the reformers' doctrine with regard to matrimony and divorce, the English Reformation did not confer on English ecclesiastical courts new powers to grant dissolution of marriages. Divorce could only be obtained by means of an act of the Parliament, and it only became of judicial competence with the creation of the Divorce Court, in 1857 — which was a civil court, not an ecclesiastical one. J. Jackson, *The Foundation and Annulment of Marriage* (London, 1951), 1 and 26. See also R.H. Helmholz, *Marriage Litigation in Medieval England* (Cambridge, 1974), 3. Moreover, it is a paradox that, on the issue of the form of marriage, the English Church remained truer to medieval canon law than did the Roman Church itself. Clandestine marriages (i.e. marriages not celebrated *in facie Ecclesiae*, "in the face of the Church") continued to be valid in post-Reformation England as they had been all over the Roman Church territories until the sixteenth century. Contrariwise, in the Catholic areas of the Continent they ceased to be valid after the Council of Trent, for the *Tametsi* decree (1563) imposed a specific public form as a necessary requirement for the valid celebration of marriage.

two legal environments were different[31]. Indeed, the lawyers who practiced in English ecclesiastical courts remained loyal to sources and methods of analysis of continental origin, despite their acceptance of parliamentary supremacy, and despite their occasional use — without any sense of being bound to do so — of common law ideas, especially after the middle of the seventeenth century[32].

The second question centers on the issue of the canon law applied by English ecclesiastical courts prior to the Reformation, more specifically, whether it was the same canon law that was being elaborated on the Continent, based on papal decretals and on the writings of the canonists. In this case, the answer is not so simple.

The debate held by Stubbs and Maitland towards the end of the last century on this issue is well known. Stubbs, Anglican bishop of Oxford, and prone to highlight the English Church's independence even prior to the Reformation, defended the autochthonous character of canon law applied by Church courts in medieval England. Obviously — he affirmed — Roman canon law was known and observed, although not by virtue of its binding nature over the English Church, but rather because of the respect it inspired as an authoritative source. It became binding only to the extent it was established by custom or ratified by national and provincial councils[33].

Contrariwise, Maitland argued in favor of the binding legislative character of the Roman Church's canon law in English ecclesiastical courts prior to the separation. He based his view on the writings of

---

[31] C.C. Langdell, "The Development of Equity Pleading from Canon Law Procedure, in *Select Essays in Anglo-American Legal History*, vol. 2, 777-778.

[32] See R.H. Helmholz, *Roman Canon Law in Reformation England*, 121-194.

[33] Stubbs' thesis can be found in his *Seventeen Lectures on the Study of Medieval and Modern History* (Oxford, 3rd ed, 1900), 351 et seq., and in his study "The History of the Canon Law in England," published in vol. 1 of *Select Essays in Anglo-American Legal History*, 248 et seq.

various English canonists — especially William Lyndwood —, on the existence and intervention of the papal judges delegate, and on the analysis of diverse confrontations between Church and State in medieval England[34].

It was Maitland's opinion that would prevail among the historians of Anglo-American law until Donahue revisited the controversy on the basis of an examination of the archives of various ecclesiastical courts, and provided new variations to Maitland's theory [35]. In brief, this North American historian concluded that English ecclesiastical courts ruled in accordance with Roman canon law, but that their decisions were often complemented by recourse to local laws and customs which resulted in several departures from their continental counterparts[36]. Helmholz reached similar conclusions in the specific field of matrimonial law, while at the same time underlining the strong influence of the canon law on the practice of ecclesiastical courts[37].

---

[34] Maitland's opinion is explained in his collection of essays published under the title of *Roman Canon Law in the Church of England* (London, 1898).

[35] C. Donahue, Jr., "Roman Canon Law in the Medieval English Church: Stubbs vs. Maitland Re-Examined After 75 Years in the Light of Some Records from the Church Courts", 72 *Michigan Law Review* 647-716 (1974). The archives used as basis for his conclusions are those of the Consistory Court of York (fourteenth century), and those of the ecclesiastical courts of Canterbury (thirteenth century).

[36] Subsequently, Donahue again has made similar statements in relation to the specific subject of the proof by witnesses in the canonical procedure: "Proof by Witnesses in the Church Courts of Medieval England: An Imperfect Reception of the Learned Law", in *On the laws and customs of England. Essays in Honor of Samuel E. Thorne* (Chapel Hill, 1981), 127-158.

[37] R.H. Helmholz, *Marriage Litigation in Medieval England*,165-187; the same author has expressed analogous views in relation to the Roman-canonical institution of "legitim" (*legitima*) and its scarce application by English ecclesiastical courts (see "Legitim in English Legal History", in *Canon Law and the Law of England*, 258 et seq. With regard to the influence

Subsequently, Helmholz revisited the issue, this time beyond the sphere of marital law, adding new nuances to Donahue's findings[38]. In summary, he emphasized that the existence of local variations in the ecclesiastical jurisdictional practice vis-à-vis "official" pontifical law was not an uncommon departure from the standard operating procedure of the ecclesiastical courts of the time. On the contrary, those local adaptations were the rule, as much in England as on the Continent. It occurred in a fashion analogous to the way academic canonists analyzed and criticized pontifical laws in the characteristic scholastic style, sometimes nearly completely changing their meaning. It is not, however, that judges and canonists did not feel themselves governed by the law of the decretals. It is rather that, contrary to the assumptions of generations of jurists educated under the influence of legal positivism, they acted with much greater freedom when interpreting legal norms. In other words, contrary to Stubbs' belief, the decretals were regarded as binding statute law, but the concept of binding statute law was much less rigid than Maitland had thought. Therefore, Helmholz has rightly concluded: "that sort of freedom, far from making the English Church insular, shows that it was fully a part of continental legal traditions"[39].

In light of the foregoing, it does not appear far-fetched to argue that the existence of local variations in England does not contradict the fundamental importance of classical canon law of Roman origin in Great Britain. The nucleus of applied canon law was undoubtedly Roman. Moreover, these variations — which, I insist, also existed in continental practice — are only of relative significance in a legal system such as canon law, which has traditionally been open to the

---

of the continental canonical collections in the kingdom of England, see C. Duggan, "The Reception of Canon Law in England in the Later-Twelfth Century", in S. Kuttner / J.J. Ryan, eds, *Proceedings of the Second International Congress of Medieval Canon Law* (E Civitate Vaticana, 1965), 359-390.

[38] R.H. Helmholz, *Roman Canon Law in Reformation England*, 4 et seq.

[39] Ibid., 19.

creation of "particular law" (*ius particulare*), whether by legal or customary channels.

Chapter 4

The Court of Chancery

The second area of significant contact between canon law and English law is the equity jurisdiction developed in the Court of Chancery.

It is not easy to define equity in a conceptual manner; it is only possible to describe it by reference to the jurisdiction which brought it to life[1]. Nor is equity a phenomenon exclusive to Anglo-American law; its origins go back to the Greek notion of *epikeia*, which was inherited by the Roman concept of *æquitas*[2]. It is not rash to venture that, in diverse forms, it is present in all legal orders[3].

---

[1] This fact is pointed out at the beginning of F.W. Maitland, *Equity. A Course of Lectures*. This book is of great utility to understand the notion of equity in England, and — as its title suggests — consists in a collection of Maitland's lectures to his Cambridge students. It was published for the first time in 1909; the edition I have used is from 1949. On the other hand, the most complete work on the Court of Chancery are still the two big volumes by G. SPENCE, *The Equitable Jurisdiction of the Court of Chancery* (Philadelphia, 1846); although it should be noted that it was written before the unification of jurisdictions in England.

[2] In regard to the different historical notions of equity in the western juridical world, see G. Broggini, "Riflessioni sull'equità", 22 *Ius* 1 et seq.

However, unlike the situation in other systems, in English law equity did not remain merely one of the abstract notions which, with varying intensity, impregnated the legal order as a whole. Quite to the contrary. Without losing its character of inspiring principle, it became a separate branch of law with its own jurisdiction and specific traits, which had a particular connection with canon law, through the Court of Chancery, during the Middle Ages.

It should be understood, however, that Chancery did not introduce the concept of equity into England. During early times, common law courts often decided cases by equity as well as according to strict law[4]. However, equity grew into a distinct branch of English law through the rise of the Court of Chancery[5]. It was an interesting historical process that is worth describing, if only briefly.

(1975), and J. Castán Tobeñas, "La equidad y sus tipos históricos", *Revista General de Legislación y Jurisprudencia* 745 et seq. (1950).

[3] In this sense, and notwithstanding the contrary opinion of Esser, I do not think that the recourse to equity is destined to disappear in a sufficiently perfected law (Esser's opinion is cited by G. Broggini, *Riflessioni sull'equità*, 41-42). I rather consider that equity does continue and will continue to be a living reality in all legal systems, including international law. In this regard, some interesting observations have been written on the function which *epikeia* can fulfil as a corrective factor of the rules — above all procedural rules — of international law: see S.W. De Vine, "Polyconnotational Equity and the Role of *Epiekeia* in International Law", 24 *Texas International Law Journal* 150-259 (1989).

[4] See H.D. Hazeltine, "The Early History of English Equity", in P. Vinogradoff, ed, *Essays in Legal History* (Oxford, 1923), 261-285; W.S. Holdsworth, "The Early History of Equity", 13 *Michigan Law Review* 293 et seq. (1915).

[5] According to G.B. Adams, "The Origin of English Equity", in E.D. Re, ed, *Selected Essays in Equity* (New York, 1955), 1 et seq., until the fourteenth century a clear distinction between common law and equity was not possible.

1. Historical Evolution

In the times immediately following the Conquest, royal courts were regarded as the only existing channel for the administration of justice in the name of the King. However, as their jurisdictional reach consolidated, particularly from the thirteenth century onward, the limitations brought on by their evolution become evident. One was their growing formalism, derived from the system of writs. But there was also the fact that the common law ruled over things — land, especially — more than over people; therefore it did not develop instruments to enforce specific performance of obligations — it had to content itself with making the wronged party whole through damages. Nor did it have any procedural methods designed to prevent illicit acts; it could only punish them. These procedural deficiencies were added to the difficulties in imparting justice that judges often experienced when they clashed with the interests of the nobility.

Under these circumstances, it became necessary to seek corrective elements. Most of these came not from within the common law, but from outside it, due to the judicial activity of the Chancery. Those who could not obtain justice in ordinary courts could resort to the prerogative of the King, who was considered the kingdom's fountain of justice. The monarch, for his part, exercised this gracious prerogative through the Chancellor, a member of the royal Council. Placing this duty on the Chancellor seemed particularly appropriate, since his office was already the central nexus in the royal system of justice by virtue of its responsibility in the issuing of writs.

Chancery thus began to provide a remedy in situations where the common law had proved ineffective. This ineffectiveness was commonly attributable to two factors: the lack of elasticity in its principles and procedure, and a disparity in position between the litigants (when a defendant was particularly powerful the ordinary courts were unable to act effectively against him)[6]. The first of these

[6] W.P. Baildon, *Select Cases in Chancery, 1364-1471* (London: Selden Society, 1896), xxi. In the same sense, W.T. Barbour, "The History of Contract in Early English Equity", in P. Vinogradoff, ed, *Oxford Studies in*

reasons would prove the most important, since, in the long run, it would give rise to what would later be termed "equitable matters", considered the exclusive competence of the Chancery.

It appears that the Chancellor acted initially as an informal delegate for the King and his Council, with no specific guide for his decisions, and was moved only by the necessity to make up for the deficiencies of the common law[7]. Later on, he would decide "according to conscience", that is to say, according to the principles of natural justice, without taking into account the norms of the common law. Such course of action can easily be understood when we observe the fact that the Chancellor — at the time almost invariably an ecclesiastic — was regarded as "keeper of the King's conscience".

In short, the aim was to revitalize the royal jurisdiction by curing the practical faults existing in the common law by recourse to superior principles which, due to their abstract character, possessed greater flexibility[8]. This has led diverse authors to see an analogy between the English equity and, the *ius honorarium* of Roman prætors[9]. In both

---

Social and Legal History, vol.4 (New York, 1974; repr. of the 1st ed, 1914), 74 et seq.

[7] See T.F.T. Plucknett, *Concise History*, 180.

[8] Baker has pointed out that the English Chancellors' recourse to conscience frequently entailed accepting the relaxation of a legal norm in order to do justice in view of the particular circumstances of the case. On the contrary, the common law judges preferred not to consider the special facts as a reason for an exception to the general rule — they decidedly favored the certainty and the clarity of the law. Hence Chancery tried successfully to correct that deficiency of the common law; and it was something that Chancery could do because it was free from the procedural formalities of the common law, it had a jurisdiction *in personam*, and its decisions were not recorded, so that it was not tied to precedent. See J.H. Baker, introduction to *The Reports of Sir John Spelman,* 37 et seq.

[9] See G. Spence, *Equitable Jurisdiction*, vol. 1, 321 et seq.; T.E. Scrutton, *The Influence of the Roman Law in the Law of England* (Cambridge, 1885), 155; W.W. Buckland / A.D. Mcnair, *Roman Law and Common Law,*

cases the rigidity and formalism of ancient law was modified by resorting to the ideal of justice represented by equity. However, contrary to what happened in Roman law, equity did not transform earlier law from the inside; rather it created a parallel and independent branch which maintained its own jurisdiction until the judicial reforms of the nineteenth century[10].

That process of materialization of equity[11] was a consequence of the remarkable and rapid increase of cases brought before the Chancellor. The group of officials assisting him eventually became the Court of Chancery. During the fourteenth century, the Court gradually consolidated its powers and, mostly as a result of the growth of its jurisdiction over uses[12], it had acquired full status as a separate court by the first third of the fifteenth century[13].

(Cambridge, 1965; 2d ed, revised by F.H. Lawson), 4 et seq.; F. Wieacker, "The Importance of Roman Law for Western Civilization and Western Legal Thought", 4 *Boston College International and Comparative Law Review* 265 et seq. (1981).

[10] The analogies and differences between the Roman *ius honorarium* and the English equity have been the subject of a careful and suggestive analysis by G. Pugliese, "*Ius honorarium* a Roma ed *equity* nei sistemi di *common law*", *Rivista Trimestrale di Diritto e Procedura Civile*1105 et seq. (1988).

[11] It is necessary to point out that, in the early centuries of its development, Chancery was conceived as a court of conscience and not as a court of equity. The change, as I shall mention later on, took place in the sixteenth century, through the influence of Saint German's work. See J.L. Barton, introduction to *St German's Doctor and Student* (London: Selden Society, 1974), xlvii.

[12] See M.E. Avery, "The History of the Equitable Jurisdiction of Chancery before 1460", 42 *Bulletin of the Institute of Historical Research* 135 et seq. (1969).

[13] It seems that the crucial moment was the multiplication of cases taken before the Chancery when John Stafford was Chancellor (1432-1450). See S.W. De Vine, "The Concept of *Epiekeia* in the Chancellor of England's Enforcement of the Feoffment to Uses before 1535", 21 *University of British Columbia Law Review* 323 et seq. (1987). Nevertheless, the year 1474 is

The sixteenth century brought about important innovations. From the point of view of the principles of equity, Protestantism would exercise important influence on the canonical notion of conscience which had inspired Chancery's decisions during the Middle Ages, despite the continuity of the medieval tradition which, as we shall see, was secured by the writings of St German[14]. Moreover, the chain of ecclesiastical Chancellors was interrupted by the appointment of Thomas More in 1529; especially from 1558 the post was almost always occupied by a common lawyer[15].

On the other hand, changes also affected the organizational aspects of equity. The expansion of the Chancery jurisdiction would be reflected in the appearance of a number of municipal equity courts[16]. And, above all, the systematic record of Chancellors' decisions, which begins under the reign of Henry VIII, laid the foundations for equity to mature into a system of legal rules of judicial origin, in a manner similar to the common law. The Court of Chancery would eventually accept the *stare decisis* doctrine, and the Chancellor came to be bound by previous decisions, in contrast with the wider discretion he had possessed in early days[17]. This "technicalization" of equity occurred mostly from the seventeenth century onwards, mainly during the rules of Chancellors Nottingham, Hardwick and Eldon[18].

---

usually mentioned as the date when the Chancellor issued a decree in his own name for the first time (see G. Pugliese, *"Ius honorarium" a Roma ed "equity" nei sistemi di common law"*, 1117, and the bibliography there cited).

[14] See D.E.D. Yale, introduction to E. Hake, *Epikeia. A dialogue on Equity in Three Parts* (New Haven, 1953), xiii et seq.

[15] Cfr. G. Pugliese, *"Ius honorarium" a Roma ed "equity"*, 1119.

[16] See T.F.T. Plucknett, *Concise History*, 671 et seq.

[17] See R. David, *Les grands sistèmes juridiques contemporains*, 338 et seq.; F. Pollock, "The Transformation of Equity", in P. Vinogradoff, ed, *Essays in Legal History* (Oxford, 1913), 286 et seq.

[18] This fact has received different appraisals by scholars. Some have noted that it was a way to remedy the frequent uncertainty of the Court's decisions,

The effects were not always positive, at least insofar as the agility with which the Chancery functioned was concerned. As Spence ironically observed of Chancery's last century: "No man, as things now stand, can enter into a Chancery suit with any reasonable hope of being alive at its termination, if he has a determined adversary"[19].

The consolidation of equity remained *in crescendo* throughout the following centuries, confirming its character as a fundamental and distinct part of the English legal system, with an independent jurisdiction. It is not surprising, therefore, that the same system would be retained in many of the English colonies in North America. On the new continent the distinction between common law and equity was preserved, and consequently they became the two lines which delimit the coordinates of Anglo-American law[20].

In England, the situation remained relatively unchanged until the legal reorganization caused by the Judicature Acts of 1873 and 1875, which merged the two branches of English law. The Court of

---

captured in a popular saying: "equity varies in accordance with the length of a Chancellor's foot" (see, for instance, G. Radbruch, *El espíritu del Derecho inglés*, 54); the origin of that saying seems to come from the British historian John Selden, in the seventeenth century (W.S. Holdsworth, *History of English Law*, vol. 1, 467-468). Contrariwise, some other authors have criticized Chancery's evolution towards what they have called a *rigor æquitatis*, comparable to the *rigor iuris* — and this is something certainly paradoxical if we bear in mind that equity arose to mitigate the formal rigidity of the common law (see V. Frosini, "La struttura del giudizio di equità", in *Teoremi e problemi di scienza giuridica* (Milano, 1971), 202 et seq.).

[19] Quoted by Baron Bowen, "Progress in the Administration of Justice during the Victorian Period", in *Select Essays in Anglo-American Legal History*, vol. 1, 529.

[20] See B.F. Brown, "Equity in the Law of the United States of America", in *Equity in the World's Legal Systems*, 205 et seq.; G. Glenn / K.R. Redden, "Equity. A Visit to the Founding Fathers", in *Selected Essays on Equity*, 15 et seq.; A.P. Sereni, *Studi di diritto comparato. I. Diritto degli Stati Uniti* (Milano, 1965), 143 et seq. Not all North-American states, however, instituted separate common law and equity courts.

Chancery lost its independence and became the Chancery Division of the High Court of Justice. Since then, any English court is entitled to apply both common law and rules of equity.

That merger, however, was primarily administrative rather than substantive. As an Italian scholar has vividly described it, both juridical "blocks" — common law and equity — subsist separately in the legal mind of Anglo-American countries[21]. Indeed the Chancery Division continues to judge over the same matters that were traditionally resolved by the Court of Chancery, and no essential changes in procedure have occurred. Furthermore, the supremacy of the principles of equity was confirmed by the Judicature Act of 1873, for it provided that, in the event of a conflict between legal and equitable rights, the latter should prevail[22]. The same can be said with regard to the United States. Despite the process of unifying jurisdictions (commenced in 1848, when the state of New York decreed the merger of the two jurisdictions), the unification has not eliminated the distinction between legal and equitable rights — the latter prevailing whenever a conflict arises, just as it does in England[23].

It is not easy to elaborate a general theory of equity, particularly since, from its birth, it developed in the same asystematic fashion as did the common law. The only guiding principle in its evolution seemed to be the aim of correcting the deficiencies of the common law, according to the criteria of justice rooted in the conscience of the

---

[21] G. Broggini, *Riflessioni sull'equità*, 31.

[22] See F.W. Maitland, *Equity,* 16.

[23] See the writings of A.P. Sereni and G. Glenn / K.R. Redden cited in note 61. In order to confirm that the distinction between these two branches of English law was transplanted to the United States, the text of the North American Constitution, article III, section 2, is very eloquent: "The judicial Power shall extend to all cases, in Law and Equity, arising under this Constitution…".

Chancellor[24]. However, it is possible to highlight its main characteristics.

First, equity was unquestionably of a complementary character in relation to the common law. The fact that equity existed as a coherent set of norms exercising a separate jurisdiction should not lead us into thinking that it was a self-sufficient system in conflict with the common law. On the contrary, its evolution presupposed the existence of the common law, which gave consistency to what would otherwise have been an amorphous assortment of rules. As Maitland wrote, "equity without common law would have been a castle in the air, an impossibility"[25]. Similarly, according to Plucknett's comparison, equity could be described as a gloss of the common law, written by English Chancellors[26]. No doubt, tensions with the common law existed throughout the history of the Court of Chancery[27]. But from the beginning, Chancellors acknowledged that they acted within the

---

[24] A Mexican scholar has described this fact very expressively: "[equity] no es una estructura hecha por legisladores teóricos o por jurisconsultos filósofos, sino, lo mismo que la *common law*, un crecimiento gradual, producto de las necesidades de una raza de hombres prácticos que se esfuerzan más bien en realizar la justicia que en ceñirse a la lógica. De ahí que este sistema jurídico de los anglosajones, según ellos mismos lo advierten, no sea un derecho ordenado conforme a un plan lógico o científico, como la legislación romana y la europea en general, sino en realidad una agrupación de doctrinas, materias y procedimientos de órdenes jurídicos diversos y desarticulados, que se han ido formando espontáneamente en la práctica, sin más norma que la de llenar los vacíos que la rama de la *common law* dejó en su trayectoria" (O. Rabasa, *El derecho angloamericano,* (Mexico, 2d ed, 1982), 151-152.

[25] F.W. Maitland, *Equity*, 19.

[26] See T.F.T. Plucknett, *Concise History*, 673.

[27] The most significant conflict arose, in 1615, between the Chancellor, Lord Ellesmere, and Sir Edward Coke, then Chief Justice of the Court of the King's Bench. King James I resolved the dispute in favor of the Chancellor, and Coke was relieved of his position in 1616.

framework of the common law — endeavouring to supplement it, not to overturn it[28].

The peculiar and fragmented growth of Chancery explains that it evolved without a wholly coherent, clearly defined jurisdiction. Certainly, there were three generic matters which came under its jurisdiction, summarized in the ancient aphorism: "These three give place in court of conscience, fraud, accident and breach of confidence". In practice, however, its jurisdiction was broad, and had an undeniable tendency to expand. It had only two clear boundaries: its circumscription to the civil domain — it never applied in criminal law — and the fact that its jurisdiction was *in personam* and not *in rem* (over persons, not over things).

As a result of this, the Court of Chancery exercised jurisdiction over a large variety of matters. Significantly, it played a pivotal role in the birth and development of the use — the predecessor of the modern day trust. However, its role also extended, with more or less intensity, to contractual law, the law of succession, guardianship, mortgages law, property of married women, and even the repression of witchcraft, to cite only a few of the more prominent examples[29].

---

[28] See in this regard, particularly in connection with the jurisdiction over uses exercised by Chancellors, the interesting observations written by S.W. De Vine, *The Concept of "Epiekeia" in the Chancellor of England's Enforcement of the Feoffment to Uses before 1535*, 329 et seq. An Italian scholar, trying to define the complementary nature of the equity, has written that its role was not to modify, correct or integrate the common law, but rather to correct and integrate its effects (T. Ravà, "Un'esperienza di interpretazione comparativa: origine e struttura delle fonti nella *common law* inglese", *Rivista di Diritto Civile* (1974), 212. On the other hand, the subsidiary character of equity is well captured in one of the maxims which describes its fundamental principles: "equity follows the law". It means that the equity court must apply the common law in those aspects of the question where no equitable rules exist.

[29] With regard to the Chancery's activity in those fields, apart from the general treatises on the history of English law already cited, and the writings of Spence and Maitland mentioned in this chapter, see: M.E. Avery, *The History of the Equitable Jurisdiction*; J.H. Baker, "Origins of the 'Doctrine'

It would be beyond the scope of this work to examine in detail the scholarly discussions regarding the exact reach of the jurisdiction historically exerted by Chancery. For our purposes it is sufficient to emphasize that, regardless of the outcome in that controversy, the activity of Chancery has left an important imprint on diverse aspects of Anglo-American law, both procedural and substantive. Examples are the affidavits and interrogatories, trial by judge alone, the examination of the parties as witnesses, most forms of relief other than damages, not to mention the current writ of the High Court, which is modelled on the *subpœna* typical of Chancery rather than the original writ of the common law[30].

At the same time, we should consider that equity played a leading role in creating certain institutions which would later be adopted by the common law. A clear example is the capacity of married women to own property — by means of the so-called "separate use" — centuries before they were given that legal capacity in 1882. The examples continue to more recent periods: the introduction of new kinds of property, such as copyright and trademarks, in the eighteenth century, before parliament took them over; or, in the last century, the recognition of joint-stock companies with limited liability before the statutory foundations on modern company law were laid in 1844 and 1856[31].

---

of Consideration", in *On the Laws and Customs of England. Essays in Honor of Samuel E. Thorne* (Chapel Hill, 1981), 336 et seq.; W.T. Barbour, *The History of Contract*, and *Some Aspects of Fifteenth Century Chancery*; J.L. Barton, *Roman Law in England*, 50 et seq., and "The Medieval Use," 81 *Law Quarterly Review* 562-577 (1965); N. Pronay, "The Chancellor, the Chancery, and the Council at the End of the Fifteenth Century", in *British Government and Administration. Studies presented to S.B. Chrimes* (Cardiff, 1974), 87-103 et seq.; T.E. Scrutton, *The Influence of the Roman Law*, 152 et seq.; S.W. De Vine, *The Concept of "Epiekeia"*; P. Vinogradoff, "Reason and Conscience in Sixteenth Century Jurisprudence", in his *Collected papers*, vol. 2 (Oxford, 1828), 190-204.

30 J.H. Baker, *An Introduction to English Legal History*, 96 et seq.

31 Ibid., 176 et seq.

Moreover, we should bear in mind that two of the most characteristic instruments of judicial power — injunction and specific performance — were born as equitable remedies, and only much later, with the merger of the two branches, did they extend to the common law courts. The first consists in a mandate by the judge ordering or prohibiting specified conduct; the addressee remains bound in such a way that his disobedience is punishable as contempt of court. This flexible and equitable remedy would be successively applied in a diversity of fields, among them contract law, with the objective of demanding the specific performance of the contract — something which remained outside the boundaries of the common law, which could only force the debtor to pay compensatory damages[32].

2. The Court of Chancery and Canon Law

The transcendent importance of equity within Anglo-American law can be deduced from the prior discussion. Just as it is unthinkable to conceive of the continental tradition without Roman law, it is impossible to understand the Anglo-American legal tradition without equity. The next logical step is now to explore the role played by canon law in this special branch of English law.

This topic has been examined by historians of law since the last century. The conclusions reached by each of them seem to be directly correlated with the researcher's views regarding the degree of insularity which guided the evolution of Anglo-American law as a whole. Thus Blackstone attributed notable weight to Roman and canon law in the formation of the principles of equity[33]. And there is

---

[32] See C.K. Allen, *Law in the Making* (Oxford, 7th ed, 1964), 578 et seq.; F.W. Maitland, *Equity,* 301 et seq.; and R. Zimmermann, *The Law of Obligations. Roman Foundations of the Civilian Tradition* (Cape Town & München, 1992), 776 et seq.

[33] Blackstone wrote: "The systems of jurisprudence in our courts both of law and equity are now equally artificial systems, founded in the same principles of justice and positive law; but varied by different usages in the forms and mode of their proceedings: the one being originally derived

in fact historical evidence which shows that, from the end of the fourteenth century, the commons regularly complained that Chancery interfered with common law and proceeded in accordance with the formalities of civil and canon law[34].

More recently, however, some of the most authoritative historians of English law, while acknowledging the important influence of foreign legal sources in the procedural aspects of the operation of the Court of Chancery, evince scepticism about the influence exerted in substantive areas of law. Baker especially contends that there is no incontestable evidence proving that Chancery applied norms taken from canon law, although its procedural practice was based on the Roman-canonical procedure rather than on the common law procedure[35]. Personally I find it difficult to believe in that sort of "legal schizophrenia" of English Chancellors: willing to proceed in accordance with the canonical procedural formalities, but reticent to apply the substantive law of the same origin — especially when they were conversant with canon law, somehow considered a "legal materialization" of the Christian conscience.

Essentially, the main difficulty in reaching an unqualified opinion is the lack of documentation which would allow researchers to understand, beyond the shadow of a doubt, what principles and doctrines served as the basis for the Chancellors' decisions during the first centuries of their judicial activity. Indeed, it is not until the reign of Henry VIII that the Chancellors' decrees and opinions are regularly and systematically recorded. Before that time we have only the

---

(though much reformed and improved) from the feudal customs, as they prevailed in different ages in the Saxon and Norman judicatures; the other (but with equal improvements) from the imperial and pontifical formularies, introduced by their clerical Chancellors" (quoted by Maitland, *Equity*, 13). Notwithstanding the quotation, Maitland himself is of the opinion that Blackstone "greatly overrates the influence of Roman and Canon law in the history of equity").

[34] J.L. Barton, "Equity in the Medieval Common Law", in *Equity in the World's Legal Systems*, 145 et seq.

[35] J.H. Baker, introduction to *The Reports of Sir John Spelman*, 26 et seq.

judgments of the Chancellors when these were endorsed on the bill, i.e. noted down on the reverse side of the petitions soliciting the intervention of the Court of Chancery — and it is rare to find these endorsements prior to the reign of Henry VI [36]. This documentary limitation obviously makes the task of tracking down the legal roots of equity more difficult, but it does not render it impossible. There is other historical evidence which, in my opinion, strongly suggests that medieval canon law significantly influenced the doctrines created by the Chancery.

First we must consider the absolute predominance of ecclesiastics among those who served as Chancellors from the birth of the Chancery through its consolidation as an independent court. I have already noted that the change whereby Chancellors began to be appointed from among common lawyers commenced with Thomas More in 1529. Prior to that date, the majority of Chancellors had been clergymen and, frequently, bishops[37].

In this regard, Maitland, sceptical about the actual qualification as canonists of many of the ecclesiastical Chancellors, contended that the medieval man of the Church was not necessarily a canonist just as he was not necessarily a saint[38]. His assertion is of course true in general terms, but there is historical evidence proving that, in its crucial period, Chancery was dominated by men who possessed an ample knowledge of canon law. Actually, many of the Chancellors

---

[36] In this regard, I cannot but recall here the valuable task of documentary reconstruction carried out by Baildon, Barbour, Avery and Pronay, whose works have previously been cited.

[37] G. Spence, *Equitable Jurisdiction*, vol. 1, 335. De Vine estimates that, of the 86 different persons who served as Chancellor between 1066 and 1535, nearly all of them were clergymen, and 60 were bishops or archbishops (S.W. De Vine, "The Franciscan Friars, the Feoffment to Uses, and Canonical Theories of Property Enjoyment before 1535", 10 *The Journal of Legal History* 1 et seq. (1989).

[38] Cited by D.E.C. Yale, introduction to A. Hake, *Epikeia. A Dialogue in Equity*, xiii.

had studied Roman and canon law — almost always at Oxford — and some had practical experience as lawyers in ecclesiastical courts.

Simpson provides very enlightening information with regard to the Chancellors of the fourteenth and beginning of the fifteenth centuries[39]. His enumeration begins with John Stafford (1432), with whom the Chancery acquires definite independence: he was bishop of Bath and Wells, and later archbishop of Canterbury, doctor in civil law from Oxford, and had been previously a practicing lawyer in the ecclesiastical courts. His successor, John Kemp (1450), archbishop of York and Canterbury, and subsequently cardinal, had also studied at Oxford and practiced as a lawyer. Thomas Bourchier (1455), archbishop of Canterbury, had graduated from the Oxford school of theology. William Waynflete (1456), archbishop of Winchester, was a doctor in civil and canon law from Oxford. George Nevill (1460) and Robert Stillington (1467) were bishops and studied at this same English university. Lawrence Booth (1473) instead studied at the University of Cambridge. Thomas Rotheram (1474), archbishop of York, possessed a doctorate in theology from Oxford, and an extensive library containing numerous works of canonists. John Russell (1483), bishop of Lincoln, was a bachelor in civil and canon law, and a doctor in canon law from Oxford. Robert Morton (1486) also possessed a bachelor's degree in both laws, and had practiced before the Chancellor's Court of Oxford, which applied civil law. Archbishop William Warham (1501), Wolsey's predecessor, had a doctorate in civil and canon law; his extensive and well-known library included a large collection of canon law books.

Likewise the clerks and officers of the Chancery involved in resolution of cases brought before the court were conversant with

---

[39] See A.W.B. Simpson, *A history of the Common Law of Contract* (Oxford, 1975), 400 et seq. As a reference book regarding the biography of British Chancellors, see the ten volumes of J. Campbell, *Lives of the Lord Chancellors and Keepers of the Great Seal of England* (there is a 2d ed, dated in Jersey, 1880).

Roman and canon law[40]. As Pronay concluded, "whatever they actually dispensed in the Court of Chancery was likely to have been a great deal more precise and juristic than *common sense and common fairness*"[41]. The entire ambience of Chancery, if we look at its relevant personnel, emanated a legal aroma of evident Roman-canonical origin. This fact becomes all the more significant given that this influence was exerted during the formative stage of that jurisdiction.

Therefore, it is not difficult to suppose that canon law was one of the sources — if not indeed the main source — that inspired the actions taken in Chancery, perhaps not always providing specific norms but definitely contributing general principles[42]. We should bear in mind that Chancellors and officials were at least as familiar with the canon law as they were with the common law. Moreover, resorting to the latter would have made no sense whatsoever, since the very purpose of Chancery's intervention was to correct the deficiencies in administration of justice occasioned by strict application of common law.

This supposition is reinforced when we consider that the Chancery characterized itself as a court of conscience[43]. At least until the

---

[40] See G. Spence, *Equitable Jurisdiction*, vol. 1, 355 et seq.; N. Pronay, *The Chancellor, the Chancery, and the Council at the End of the Fifteenth Century*, 90 et seq.

[41] Ibid., 92. Langdell pointed out that the figure of the Chancery's registrar was inspired by a similar figure existent in the ecclesiastical courts, in whose office all documents relating to the work of the court were recorded (C.C. Langdell, *The Development of Equity Pleading*, 777).

[42] Maine, in his classic work *Ancient Law*, affirms that Chancery drew its inspiration, first from canon law, later from the *ius civile* and, in the eighteenth century, from the treatises of ethics and legal philosophy elaborated by Dutch authors (cited by Scrutton, *The Influence of the Roman Law*, 155-156).

[43] It has been discussed whether the characterization of Chancery as a court of conscience meant that the Chancellor decided according to his own conscience, or rather that the purpose of his action was to enforce the

seventeenth century, the Chancellor had almost unfettered discretion to decide the cases presented before him. His only guide was "conscience"[44], and conscience then implied abiding by principles of natural justice and moral criteria, in their Christian interpretation, which were supposed to have a particular materialization in the law of the Church[45].

With regard to the canonical texts that may have served as foundation for the decisions, it is worth recalling that many of the Chancellors, by virtue of having studied at Oxford, would have been

---

defendant's duties of conscience. I think that, in reality, they are the two sides of the same coin, as the central issue was to transfer the duties of natural justice to the judicial domain, where they could be subject to the Chancellor's coercive power. Probably to describe Chancery as a court of conscience meant primarily that it was directed to render judicially enforceable some personal obligations which were considered substantially moral and not legal, i.e. they could not be enforced by the common law courts and therefore the wronged person did not have a legal remedy. However, to that purpose, the Chancellor had to resort to his own conscience, which permitted him to discern when and up to what extent the fulfilment of those moral duties was to be enforced (with regard to the Chancellor's conscience, see A.W.B. Simpson, *A History of the Common Law of Contract*, 396 et seq.).

[44] After a detailed analysis of the cases brought before the Court of Chancery between 1364 and 1471, Baildon notes that the grounds alleged as a basis in the petitions to the Chancellor were nearly always expressed with the words "conscience", "good faith", "reason", or similar expressions. Rarely does the term "equity" appear: instead it became commonplace from the sixteenth century, largely due to the influence of St. German's books (W.P. Baildon, *Select Cases in Chancery*, xxix-xxx). On the other hand, it is worth recalling here a statement contained in one of the Year Books of Henry IV's reign, according to which the Chancellor decides "secundum conscientiam et non secundum allegata" (Y.B. 9. Edw.IV, 14.9, cited by W. Barbour, *Some Aspects of Fifteenth Century Chancery*, 854).

[45] See J.L. Barton's introduction to the edition of *St. German's Doctor and Student*, xxix et seq. Spence is very conclusive in maintaining that the recourse to conscience as a principle of decision — which was something unknown to the common law — was an invention of ecclesiastical Chancellors (*Equitable Jurisdiction*, vol. 1, 410).

well acquainted with the medieval canonical collections. Moreover, it is documented that, from the twelfth century and especially after the arrival of Vacarius, the works of continental canonists were relatively widespread in the British Isles; there were also frequent exchanges of professors and students between universities on either side of the Channel[46]. In addition, Maitland attributes the principal influence of canonical thought on equity to the Chancellors' familiarity with the *regulæ iuris* included at the end of the Boniface VIII's *Liber Sextus*[47]. This can be clearly seen by comparing some of those concise "rules of law" with the maxims of equity through which historian have sought to describe the fundamental principles behind the Chancery's decisions[48]. .

---

[46] See C. Duggan, "The Reception of Canon Law in England in the Later-Twelfth Century", in S. Kuttner / J.J. Ryan, eds, *Proceedings of the Second International Congress of Medieval Canon law* (E Civitate Vaticana, 1965), 359-390; S. Kuttner / E. Rathbone, "Anglo-American Canonists of the Twelfth Century", 7 *Traditio* , 279-358 (1949-51).

[47] F.W. Maitland, *Equity,* 8.

[48] There is no unanimous agreement about the exact number of the equity maxims. The first book on the subject was seemingly published by Richard Francis in 1727, under the title of *Maxims of Equity Collected from and Proved by Cases, out of the Books of the best Authority, in the High Court of Chancery*; it included fourteen maxims. Other authors report a different number of maxims, in some cases reaching as many as twenty. However, there are twelve fundamental maxims universally accepted. In these pages, other than Francis' book, I have followed the exposition of M. Garsia, *Equity in a nutshell* (London, 3rd ed, 1941), 9 et seq. With regard to the origin and significance of the maxims of equity, and their use by North American judicature, see R. Pound, "On Certain Maxims of Equity", in *Cambridge Legal Essays Written in Honor of and Presented to Doctor Bond, Professor Buckland and Professor Kenny* (Cambridge, 1926), 259-277; J. Story, *Commentaries on Equity Jurisprudence as Administered in England and America,* vol. 1, (Boston, 5th ed, 1849), 66 et seq.

It is important to note that, in the tradition of English law, enormous value is given to the maxims: they are considered indubitable truths that require no justification. See R. Pound, "The Maxims of Equity, I: Of Maxims

For example, the rule *qui prior est tempore potior est iure* has a virtually literal parallel in the maxim "where equities are equal the first in time shall prevail". Likewise, the maxim "equity will not suffer a wrong to be without a remedy" seems to reflect the *regulæ iuris* according to which *possessor malæ fidei ullo tempore non præscribit* and *pro possessore habetur qui dolo desiit possidere*. In the same way, one can compare the notion of equality before the law, contained in the maxim "equality is equity", and in the rule *in iudiciis non est acceptio personarum habenda*. Or we can compare also the negative effects deriving from a lack of diligence which are expressed in the maxim "delay defeats equity", and in the rule *damnum, quod quis sua culpa sentit, sibi debet, non aliis, imputare*. Something similar can be affirmed on the effects of bad faith: it is not difficult to perceive the resemblance between the rule *frustra sibi fidem quis postulat ab eo servari, cui fidem a se præstitam servare recusat,* and the maxims "he that has committed iniquity, shall not have equity" and "he that will have equity done to him, must do it to the same person". Finally, there is a equivalent parallel concerning unjust enrichment between the rule *locupletari non debet aliquis cum alterius iniuria vel iactura* and the maxims "it is equity that he should make satisfaction, who received the benefit" and "it is equity that he should have satisfaction, who sustained the loss"[49].

Generally", 34 *Harvard Law Review*, 809-836 (1921); regrettably the author never came to publish the announced second part of that work, destined to the specific study of the maxims within the system of equitable jurisdiction. See also P. Stein, *Regulæ Iuris. From Juristic Rules to Legal Maxims* (Edinburgh, 1966); P. Vinogradoff, "Les maximes dans l'ancien Droit Commune anglais", in *Collected papers*, vol. 2 (Oxford, 1928), 239-247; J. Williams, "Latin Maxims in English Law", 20 *Law Magazine and Law Review* 283-295 (1894-1895). Some of these works — especially the one by Stein — contain interesting remarks in relation to the origin of the *regulæ iuris* of the *Liber Sextus* and its importance in English law.

[49] For the exposition of the *regulæ iuris* of the *Liber Sextus* I have followed the edition of the *Corpus Iuris Canonici* prepared by Richter / Friedberg, vol. 2 (Graz, 1955), 1122-1124. The numbers of the rules cited are, in order of quotation: 54, 2, 36, 12, 86, 75 and 48.

That presumptive link between the principles of canon law and Chancery's maxims has led many scholars to consider the probability of a historical connection between English equity and *æquitas canonica*. This is a notion which, as Calasso has written, synthesizes the ideological world of the Middle Ages, and is to be found at the root of its entire legal system — in the legislative norms as well as in the doctrinal constructs[50]. Indeed, the concept of *æquitas canonica* is the product of a transformation of the Greek and Roman heritage by the spirit of medieval Christendom, and occupies an important position among the writings of the canonists of the classical era. It is treated as a necessary element of justice, which itself needs to take into account the circumstances of each case to correct the unavoidable imperfection implicit in the general character of the law[51].

The notion that *æquitas canonica* may have influenced the principles governing the actions of English Chancellors takes on a special interest when we analyze a valuable piece of historical testimony: one of the writings of Christopher St. German which was

[50] F. Calasso, *Medio Evo del Diritto*, 324 et seq. Such a connection between equity and *æquitas canonica* is principally due to the writings of St. German, which will be mentioned forthwith. In addition to the works which I shall cite later on, I must name here the unpublished doctoral thesis presented in The University of Navarra by A. Portolés, *"Æquitas canonica" y "equity"*, 1977.

[51] Canon law modified the notion of equity inherited from the Greeks and Romans by adding different duties derived from the Christian conscience. From a general point of view it contributed the idea of mercy, and from a more specific perspective, the protection of the poor and needy, as well as the legal enforceability of the relations of confidence. With regard to the concept of canonical equity in the writings of the first canonists of the classical period, see J. Gaudemet, "Équité et droit chez Gratian et les premiers décrétistes", in *La storia del diritto nel quadro delle scienze storiche* (Firenze, 1966), 269 et seq. For a broader view of equity in canon law, see P. Fedele, "L'equità canonica", within his collection of writings *Discorsi sul diritto canonico* (Roma, 1973), 69 et seq.; and R. Navarro-Valls, *Equidad y revisión del derecho canónico*, an unpublished work which I have been able to read by courtesy of the author.

widely distributed and which became the starting point for a whole series of subsequent treatises dealing with equity and common law[52]. Moreover, it was written precisely during the times when the Court of Chancery had already become established as an independent court, thus beginning a new stage in its evolution.

St. German was an English lawyer of great prestige among his contemporaries, and became particularly celebrated for his debates with Thomas More over theological issues[53]. In 1523, he published in Latin his *Dialogus de Fundamentis Legum Angliæ et de Conscientia*. Seven years later he wrote a second dialogue on the same subject, and in 1613 the first English edition containing both dialogues was published. It is commonly referred to by the name of *Doctor and Student*, but its complete title was *The Dialogue in English between a Doctor of Divinitie, and a Student in the Laws of England.*

Indeed the book consists of a fictitious dialogue between a law student and a doctor in theology, through which the author seeks to unveil the central principles of English law. Without doubt, the work is a treatise on common law rather than on equity. However, the numerous references to the practice of Chancery vis-à-vis that of common law courts, and its subsequent influence on the Court of Chancery, make it a very valuable document in the study of the doctrinal foundations of English equity.

---

[52] In relation to the life and work of St. German, there are two very interesting writings: J.L. Barton's introduction to the edition of *Doctor and Student* prepared by himself and Plucknett for the Selden Society, 1974 (that is the edition which I have used here); and J.A. Guy, *Christopher St. German on Chancery and Statute* (London: Selden Society, 1985). See also J.H. Baker, introduction to *Doctor and Student* (Alabama: The Legal Classics Library, 1988); and S.E. Thorne, "*St. German's Doctor and Student*", in *The Library*, 4th series, vol. 10, 420 et seq. (1930).

[53] The context and the consequences of these controversies have been well described in the extensive introduction to *The Debellation of Salem and Bizance*, vol. 10 of "The complete works of Thomas More", ed. by J. Guy / R. Keen / C.H. Miller / R. McGugan (London, 1987).

The opening chapters of the first dialogue[54] are of particular interest. St. German commences with an explanation of the concepts of "law eternal" and "law of nature" — rather the "law of reason" — and of the six fundamentals on which he claims the law of England is based[55]. He then comments on the concepts of synderesis, reason, conscience and equity. The entire dissertation is conducted in the style of the scholastic philosophy and theology proper to the Middle Ages. However, the scholastic influence is not limited to the style, but can also be observed in the substantive ideas expressed therein.

In this regard, Vinogradoff pointed out the connections between the thinking of St. German and the works of various moralists — particularly John Gerson, John Baptist of Sales and Angelo Carleto of Clavasio[56]. This ecclesiastical influence extended not only to theoretical constructs; it can also be observed in specific legal areas in which the Chancery had performed a corrective function for the common law, especially the validity of informal contracts[57]. Subsequently, and along the same lines, De Luca has emphasized that the concept of equity adopted by St. German substantially coincides with the traditional definition of canonical *æquitas* contained in the *Summa Hostiensis*, the origins of which have been attributed to

---

[54] Chapters 1-18. Significantly, it is the Doctor of theology who leads the conversation.

[55] These six fundamentals are: the law of reason, the divine law, the general customs of the realm, the legal maxims, the particular customs of cities and towns, and the statutes approved by Parliament. The authority of the maxims is stressed with the following words: "Maxima vocantur que semper habita et tenta sunt pro lege in hoc regno [anglie] quibus non est licitum alicui legis perito contradicere quia unumquodque maximorum illorum est sibi ipsi fides" (beginning of chapter 8, pages 56-58 of the Selden Society edition).

[56] See P. Vinogradoff, "Reason and Conscience in Sixteenth-Century Jurisprudence", in his *Collected Papers*, vol. 2 (Oxford, 1928), 190 et seq.

[57] In the area of the law of contract, St. German's connections with the works of various moralists have been studied in detail by A.W.B. Simpson, *A History of the Common Law of Contract*, 377 et seq.

different canonists: "Æquitas est iustitia pensatis omnibus circumstantiis particularibus dulcore misericordiæ temperata"[58].

While some scholars have emphasized St. German's deviations from theologians and canonists[59], it is beyond question that he found his inspiration in the medieval canon law as far as his ideas on equity and conscience are concerned. This fact is of particular significance, given the extraordinary diffusion and impact which *Doctor and Student* had in legal circles of the time[60]. We should bear in mind that, according to Donahue, part of St. German's achievement was to offer a theoretical justification for the place of Chancery in English law, since in many ways it clashed with the practices of the common law[61]. That justification came through the connection of the concept of equity with the concept of conscience, all in the context of seeking to interpret law in the light of moral principles. Chancery would eventually acquire a certain exclusivity over the definition of equity, maintaining that equity could only be administered in Chancery, since it proceeded not from the common law, but rather — as in previous centuries — from the Chancellor's conscience[62]. For this reason it has

---

[58] L. De Luca, "Æquitas canonica ed equity inglese alla luce del pensiero di C. Saint German", *Ephemerides Iuris Canonici* 46 et seq. (1947). That definition is at the beginning of chapter 14 of *Doctor and Student* (page 94 of the Selden Society edition).

[59] See Z. Rueger, "Gerson's Concept of Equity and Christopher St. German", in *History of Political Thought*, vol. 3, 1-30 (1982).

[60] Its diffusion was due, among other reasons, to the fact that the theological and canonical concepts were set out in a terminology familiar to common lawyers.

[61] C. Donahue, Jr., review to the edition of *Doctor and Student* prepared for the Selden Society by T.F.T. Plucknett / J.L. Barton, 47 *Tijschrift voor Rechtsgeschiedenis* 182-186 (1979).

[62] Z. Zueger, *Gerson's Concept of Equity and Christopher St. German*, 28 et seq. The author notes the paradox that St. German's purpose was to defend the idea that equity could be applied by the common law courts — hence his emphasis on affirming that human law was subject to the law of reason, from which equity ultimately emanates. Nevertheless history walked in the opposite

been said that, if the Court of Chancery ended up being characterized as a court of equity and not as a court of conscience, it was by virtue of the works of St. German[63].

Furthermore, the publication of *Doctor and Student* occurred at a crucial time for the history of Chancery, when the office of Chancellor passed from being occupied mostly by ecclesiastics to becoming a province of the common lawyers. Thus it was assured that the Chancery would continue to be influenced by the same canonical principles which had constituted the doctrinal base of equity until then[64]. This is the reason that Vinogradoff affirmed that St. German's writings generated "a process of indirect reception of canon law" within English legal institutions[65].

These observations allow us to assert, with a high degree of probability, that principles drawn from the canon law had a marked influence on the substantive law applied by the Court of Chancery during the first centuries of its history. This high probability becomes a virtual certainty when we consider procedural practice.

It is beyond doubt that the procedure followed by the Court of Chancery was essentially different from that applied by the common law courts[66], and also more effective in many ways[67]. Especially by

---

direction: equity ceased to be applied by the common law courts and became the exclusive territory of Chancery jurisdiction.

[63] J.L. Barton, introduction to *Doctor and Student*, xlvii.

[64] S.E. Thorne, *St. German's "Doctor and Student"*, 421; D.E.C. Yale, introduction to E. Hake, *Epikeia*, xiv et seq. Holdsworth maintains that St. German did with Gerson the same as Bracton did with Azo: both authors achieved a reception of principles alien to the common law, adapting them to the peculiarities of the English legal environment (W.S. Holdsworth , "The Early History of Equity", 13 *Michigan Law Review* 296 (1915).

[65] P. Vinogradoff, *Reason and Conscience*, 198.

[66] See a detailed exposition of the Chancery procedure in: W.P. Baildon, introduction to *Select Cases in Chancery*; G. Gilbert, *The History and Practice of the High Court of Chancery* (London, 1758), especially the first part, entitled *Forum Romanum*; G. Spence, *Equitable Jurisdiction*, vol.1, 366

virtue of the unification of jurisdictions, it has contributed important elements to Anglo-American procedural law[68].

It is true that Wohlhaupter has claimed that the procedural norms of the Chancery derived from Germanic models[69]. However, his opinion has remained unique among the Anglo-American legal historians, who almost unanimously have recognized — to a lesser or a greater degree — the Roman and canonical roots of Chancery procedure.

Thus Gilbert, in the eighteenth century, pointed out numerous details in equity procedure where he observed the influence of canon law[70]: the form and effects of the writ of summons; the consequences of a defendant's non appearance; the use of the *subpœna*[71], the *reconventio*; the *litis contestatio*; the third party impleader; declinatory, peremptory, or dilatory exceptions; the interrogation of witnesses via commissions when they were far from the place of the court; the method of interrogating witnesses in secret and recording their testimony in the form of *depositiones* which were subsequently made public. Langdell has stressed this last point, adding that

---

et seq. According to Spence, the characteristic Chancery procedure was preserved, to a great extent, because the ecclesiastical Chancellors decidedly resisted the introduction of the pleading system typical of the common law. Had they ceded — he adds — much of the court's usefulness would have been lost.

[67] See M.E. Avery, *The History of the Equitable Jurisdiction*, 134 et seq.; and W. Barbour, *Some Aspects of Fifteenth Century Chancery*, 842 et seq.

[68] See, in this same chapter, notes 71-73 and accompanying text.

[69] E. Wohlaupter, "Der Einfluss naturrechtlicher und kanonistischer Gedanken auf die Entwicklung der englischen Equity", in *Acta Congressus Iuridici Internationalis*, vol. 2, (Romæ, 1935), 443.

[70] See G. Gilbert, *Forum Romanum*.

[71] The *subpœna* was the writ emanating from the Chancellor in response to the plaintiff's petition. Through it, the defendant was ordered to appear before the court, under threat of diverse sanctions — including arrest — if he refused without a reasonable cause.

Chancery borrowed the practice of interrogating witnesses under oath from canon law, something not found in the practice of the common law[72].

In order to determine more accurately the canonical origin of Chancery's procedure, De Luca compared the dialogues of St. German with the *Summa Hostientis*. He reached the conclusion that it was taken over from a peculiar institution of canon law: the *imploratio officii iudicis per modum denunciationis* — or, more briefly, the *denunciatio iudicialis privata* — which was in turn the product of the evolution experienced by an earlier canonical institution to which it bears a strong resemblance, the *denunciatio evangelica*[73]. To prove his point, De Luca noted two characteristics which thoroughly coincided with the procedural praxis followed by Chancellors, which were opposed to what was observed by the common law courts. On the one hand, the procedure began with an *imploratio* of the *officium iudicis*, which consisted of a general complaint against an allegedly illegal action (in common law courts it was not possible to initiate the trial without previously having obtained the corresponding specific writ for that case). The plaintiff then asked the court to require the defendant to desist from his illicit conduct through the imposition of a penalty. Moreover, the *denunciatio privata* sought not only to satisfy a private interest, but to repress illicit acts, with a marked penitential purpose. At this point the parallelism with the Court of Chancery is doubly apparent, as it performed a preventive and protective function, beyond the simply

---

[72] C.C. Langdell, "The Development of Equity Pleading from Canon Law Procedure", in *Select Essays in Anglo-American Legal History*, vol. 2, (Boston, 1908), 773. Of the same opinion is O.W. Holmes, "Early English Equity", in *Collected legal papers* (New York, 1920), 1 et seq.

[73] With regard to the origin and characteristics of the *denunciatio evangelica* and the *denunciatio iudicialis privata*, their reciprocal relation and the role they played in medieval canon law, see the documented work of P. Bellini, *"Denunciatio evangelica" e "Denunciatio iudicialis privata". Un capitolo di storia disciplinare della Chiesa* (Milano, 1968).

deciding a controversy, the characteristic goal of common law courts[74].

Subsequently, De Lucas' thesis has been complemented by Coing, who, with recourse to broader documentary support, has stressed the fact that the influence of the *denunciatio evangelica* in Chancery went beyond the strictly procedural environment[75]. After demonstrating that a causal connection between *denunciatio* and equity procedure was historically very likely[76], Coing noted important analogies between both styles of administering justice. In brief, these are the supplementary character in relation to ordinary jurisdiction, the use of substantive norms based on reason and conscience, and the emphasis placed on the parties' good faith.

A more detailed comparison reveals a significant resemblance from a procedural perspective. Under canon law, the plaintiff's criminal behaviour could constitute an obstacle to his recourse to the *denunciatio*, while in the equity there was a maxim which stated that "he who seeks equity must come with clean hands". Moreover, both the ecclesiastical judge and the Chancellor played an active role in the establishment of the facts, without being bound by the precise terms of the pleadings. Furthermore, under both systems the defendant had an obligation to answer each of the questions raised by the plaintiff, and the interrogation of the witnesses followed a set of questions prepared by the parties, who were not permitted to be present during interrogation. Finally, we should note that the application of the *denunciatio evangelica* to *miserabiles personæ* (the poor and the

---

[74] See L. De Luca, *Æquitas canonica ed equity inglese*, 63 et seq.

[75] H.Coing, "English Equity and the *denunciatio evangelica* of the Canon Law", 71 *Law Quarterly Review* 223-241 (1955).

[76] Coing indicates that the *denunciatio*, according to Bartollo, was of everyday use in the fourteenth century, but that it had already been fully developed in the thirteenth century. Considering that the Chancery jurisdiction became established during the fourteenth century, and in light of the canonical pedigree of most Chancellors, it is not difficult to presume that the *denunciatio* had a decisive influence on the English equity procedure.

weak) is mirrored in the perception of Chancery as "refuge of the poor and the afflicted", reflected in that court's special availability to plaintiffs arriving *in forma pauperis*[77]. This fact is particularly interesting because such jurisdiction was not exercised by the Church courts in England; it seems that this canonical principle was directly assimilated by English equity, without any mediation whatsoever from ecclesiastical jurisdiction.

Beyond mere procedure, Coing pointed out certain aspects of substantive law in which the *denunciatio* appears to have guided the practice of Chancery — especially two principles pertaining to contractual obligations. First, the canonical rule *frangenti fidem fides non est servanda*, which was opposed to the standards of Roman law, implied that a contract could be rescinded in case of breach by the other party[78]; this ground was used on numerous occasions by the Chancellor to grant rescission[79]. Second, there was an evident parallel between the regular use of specific performance and the canonical principle that it was not possible to absolve the penitent until he had complied with his promise.

The data examined so far thus seem to indicate that Chancery owed a great debt to the legal system of the medieval Church, as much in substance as in procedure. Without it, the evolution of the Court of Chancery would have very likely been different.

Naturally, it cannot be said that English equity was a mere copy of continental canon law. Quite to the contrary, despite all their faults, the merit of English Chancellors consisted in knowing how to employ the canon law — a learned law, to a great extent elaborated in Universities — to shape and give new form to an existing jurisdiction which they exercised on behalf of the Crown in order to overcome

---

[77] See G. Spence, *Equitable Jurisdiction*, vol. 1, 386. In regard to the protection of *miserabiles personæ* by ecclesiastical jurisdiction during the Middle Ages, see R.H. Helmholz, *The Spirit of Classical Canon Law*, 116 et seq.

[78] See R. Zimmermann, *The Law of Obligations*, 800 et seq.

[79] See the cases cited by W.T. Barbour, *The History of Contract*, 123.

shortcomings in the royal system of justice. They were not just imitators. They were, in truth, creators of a new branch of English law, which sprang from sources of seemingly superior quality within the western legal tradition.

This is the reason why Coing could write that, although canon law provided the guiding principles, English equity as a differentiated legal branch was an expression of the English genius. This fact — he adds — illustrates a truth, that European civilization is based on what diverse nations have built upon a common heritage: ancient thought and Christian faith[80].

[80] H. Coing, *English Equity and the "denunciatio evangelica"*, 240.

Chapter 5

Jurisprudence or Legal Doctrine

Thus far, we have analyzed two routes by which canon law penetrated into England: the ecclesiastical courts and the Court of Chancery. Both were specific institutions that left a tangible imprint on English law which is relatively easy to identify. However, the third of the principal channels of entry is of a more abstract nature; its precise influence on positive law is harder to isolate: jurisprudence, a term which in the Anglo-American tradition has a meaning approximately equivalent to the concept which continental scholars would normally refer to as "legal doctrine" or legal science[1].

The peculiar and manifold functions fulfilled by jurisprudence are precisely what make it difficult to quantify its importance in configuring a legal system. Yet it has proved decisive throughout the history of any system with even a minimum level of development[2]. In

---

[1] In the continental legal tradition, the word jurisprudence usually designates the doctrine emanating from the decisions of the courts, and not the doctrine of legal scholars. In both traditions, however, the term gets its meaning from its Latin roots: *prudentia iuris*, i.e. practical legal wisdom.

[2] For example, some legal orders include doctrine among the sources of law. Among them is canon law: see canon 19 of the *Codex Iuris Canonici* of 1983, where, in accordance with the heritage received from the medieval *ius commune*, "the common and constant opinion of learned persons (*doctores*)"

the interaction of the diverse forces which converge in the progress of a legal order, it is hard to overestimate how judges and legislators — who have the primary responsibility for defining what positive (enforceable) law is — are influenced by those commonly shared ideas about law that constitute a sort of general "legal atmosphere", within which society breathes and lives[3]. And that legal atmosphere results to a great extent from the work of those persons whom — instinctively and inexorably — the legal conscience of a society treats as authorities.

The aforesaid is so certain that it is impossible to understand the evolution of western legal systems without reference to the jurists who, through each stage of its growth, mad their own theoretical contributions [4]. By way of example, we could note that continental law would not be the same without the work of the Roman jurisconsults, the glossators and commentators, the rationalist school of natural law, the codification movement, the German historical school of law, or the jurisprudence of concepts. And, as far as Anglo-American law is concerned, we need only refer to authors such as Bracton, St. German, Coke or Blackstone to understand how

is mentioned among the "supplementary law" or sources to be resorted to when there is a so-called "lacuna" or gap in the legal system.

[3] Perhaps it is worth mentioning an example of that influence, related to the subject of this study: a case resolved by the King's Bench in 1469, which reveals that the common law judges did not limit themselves to follow uncritically — as a sort of routine — the doctrine of precedent, but rather they had already started to construct a theoretical foundation of *stare decisis*, according to the guidelines laid out by continental jurists. In his decision of that case, judge Yelverton declared that, when a new case arrives before the court, the judge has to act as the canonists and civilians do: they must resort to the natural law, aware of the great responsibility weighing upon them, since their decision will be considered as the law in the future. The case is cited by C.K. Allen, *Law in the Making* (Oxford, 7th ed, 1964), 197-198.

[4] An example of a suggestive interpretation of the history of a legal system in the light of jurisprudence, within the Anglo-American tradition, is the book of G. Gilmore, *The Ages of American Law* (New Haven, 1977).

important jurisprudence is in shaping determined ways of looking at the law.

It is therefore not pointless to inquire into the intensity and extent to which English jurists assimilated the legal concepts developed by canon law on the Continent. In this regard, Stein has noted two periods during which continental legal ideas had ample application in the British Isles[5]. First, the twelfth and thirteenth centuries — the time of Glanvill and Bracton. Second, the first half of the sixteenth century, when, through the influence of Renaissance, England experienced a notable attraction towards a legal system that was more cosmopolitan than the common law. The following pages are mainly focused on these two periods. Nevertheless, I must allude also to the impact that the rationalist school of natural law had on Anglo-American legal thought, particularly in the United States during the nineteenth century[6]; we ought not forget that this school of thought was in turn deeply influenced by the writings produced by the Spanish scholasticism of the sixteenth and seventeenth centuries[7].

---

[5] P. Stein, *The Character and Influence of the Roman Civil Law* (London, 1988), 209 et seq. Naturally, civil lawyers have also experienced a strong and increasing attraction towards Anglo-American legal developments, especially in the last century. The writings of continental jurists cited up to now are a clear sample of that interest. To them we can add the brief but expressive account of the Anglo-American legal philosophy written by G. Radbruch, "La théorie anglo-americaine du Droit vue par un juriste du Continent", 6 *Archives de Philosophie du Droit et de Sociologie juridique* 29-45 (1936).

[6] See M.H. Hoeflich, *Roman and Civil Law and the Development of Anglo-American Jurisprudence in the Nineteenth Century* (Athens, Georgia, 1997).

[7] See F. Wieacker, "The Importance of Roman Law for Western Civilization and Western Legal Thought", 4 *Boston College International and Comparative Law Review* 260 et seq. (1981). In relation to the imprint left by the doctrine of natural law on the specific domain of the common law of contracts, with particular reference to Thomistic doctrine, to Spanish scholasticism, and to the rationalist school of natural law, see J. Gordley, "Natural Law Origins of the Common Law of Contract", in J. Barton ed, *Towards a General Law of Contract* (Berlin, 1990), 367-465. Professor

As far as the first of the two periods is concerned, I have already mentioned that the arrival of Vacarius gave rise to an extraordinary and rapid diffusion of the "learned laws" in England[8], with the result that it is possible to identify an Anglo-Norman school of canonists in the twelfth and thirteenth centuries, a school that produced figures of special merit[9]. With Oxford as a focal point, an exponential growth in numbers of canonists and civilians occurred. They held the principal positions in ecclesiastical courts and later in the Court of Chancery. It is within that cultural framework that the two first systematic treatises on common law were written: the *Tractatus de legibus et consuetudinibus regni Angliæ,* ascribed to Ranulf de Glanvill, between 1187 and 1189; and *De legibus et consuetudinibus Angliæ*, ascribed to Henry Bracton, the date of which is set at the years 1220 or 1230 by most recent studies[10].

Gordley later published an expanded version of his ideas in his monograph *The Philosophical Origins of Modern Contract Doctrine* (Oxford, 1991); I thank the author for his kindness in having permitted me to use the original unpublished typescript. More recently, through a detailed analysis of the corresponding reports, the influence of civil law on the American law immediately following Independence has been recently reassessed by R.H. Helmholz, "Use of the Civil Law in Post-Revolutionary American Jurisprudence", 66 *Tulane Law Review* 1649 et seq. (1992).

[8] With regard to the influence of Vacarius on English legal circles, see P. Stein, *The Character and Influence of the Roman Civil Law*, 167 et seq.

[9] See S. Kuttner / E. Rathbone, "Anglo-Norman Canonists of the Twelfth Century", 7 *Traditio* 279 et seq. (1949-51).

[10] Traditionally it had been thought that Bracton wrote his treatise between 1256 and 1259 (see J.H. Baker, *An Introduction to English Legal History*, 161). I would cite here two editions of Glanvill's book: the edition prepared by G.E. Woodbine for the University of Yale (New Haven, 1932), and that of G.D.G. Hall for the Selden Society (London, 1965); the latter includes an English translation of the original Latin version. The best edition of Bracton's is probably the one prepared by S.E. Thorne for the University of Harvard, in collaboration with the Selden Society (Cambridge, Mass., 1968); it is based on a revision of the edition prepared by Woodbine for the University of Yale

Glanvill, justiciar of Henry II, was an important figure in the political and legal life of his time[11]. Insofar as we are concerned here, various Roman and canonical texts could have had an influence on his treatise: the *Corpus iuris civilis* (or one of its abridged versions), Gratian's *Decretum*, the *summæ* of the first decretists, and the summaries of the Roman-canonical procedure known by the name of *ordines iudiciarii*[12]. There has been, however, some more detailed discussion over the actual influence of continental law upon Glanvill.

Scrutton considers that the continental influence was mainly terminological, and in his opinion Glanvill's work is an example of the quasi-absolute autonomy of English law with respect to the *ius utrumque* at the time[13]. Van Caenegem essentially agrees with that opinion, though he recognizes some contributions for which Glanvill seems to have been indebted to canon law. In particular, he refers to the influence of ecclesiastical concepts on the chapters dedicated by Glanvill to the testament, and the norms regarding the disqualification of members of the jury, which seems to be borrowed from the canonical rules concerning the rejection of witnesses[14]. More recently, however, Donahue reassessed the influence of the *utrumque ius* on Glanvill, especially on the systematic and methodological aspects of his treatise[15]. He would give greater weight to possible canonical influence.

(New Haven, 1915), adding an interesting preface and a translation of Bracton's Latin text into English.

[11] On the life and work of Glanvill see J.C. Russell, "Ranulf de Glanville", 45 *Speculum* 69-79 (1970).

[12] See R. Van Caenegem, *Royal writs in England from the Conquest to Glanvill* (London: Selden Society, 1959), 372-373. See also the introduction of G.D. Hall to the edition of Glanvill's treatise, previously cited, pages xxxiii et seq.

[13] T.E. Scrutton, *The Influence of the Roman Law*, 74 et seq.

[14] R. Van Caenegem, *Royal Writs in England*, 380.

[15] C. Donahue, Jr., "Ius commune, Canon Law, and Common Law in England", 66 *Tulane Law Review* 1751 et seq. (1992).

There has been less controversy about the inclination towards Roman-canonical law in the work of Bracton, perhaps because of his ecclesiastical status. The depth of that inclination has long since attracted the attention of Anglo-American historians. However, they disagree as to its exact extent[16]. On the whole, the romanistic "flavor" that impregnates the treatise is nevertheless indisputable.

Bracton's knowledge of continental law was evidently extensive, and derived from the *Corpus iuris canonici*, from Gratian's *Decretum*, and above all from Azo's *Summa*. This can be seen by his abundant use of Roman-canonical sources[17]. It is indubitable that considerable parts of his writing were inspired by the Roman and canon law of his time, especially the political sections[18] and those relating to matters of

---

[16] In relation to that controversy, Scrutton has expressively affirmed: "where authorities differ so widely, a decided answer seems hardly possible" (*The Influence of Roman Law*, 79). Apart from the aforementioned work of Scrutton, an extensive study of the influence of Roman law on Bracton, has been achieved by J.L. Barton, "Bracton as a Civilian", 42 *Tulane Law Review* 555 et seq. (1969). See also J.L. Barton, *Roman Law in England*, 13 et seq.; M. Franklin, "Bracton, Para-Bracton and the Vicarage of the Roman Law", 42 *Tulane Law Review* 455 et seq. (1969); and P. Vinogradoff, *Roman Law in Medieval Europe* (Oxford, 2d ed, 1929), 101 et seq.

[17] See S.E. Thorne's introduction to the edition of Bracton's treatise published by Harvard University Press in 1968, pages xxxvi et seq.; see also C. Donahue, Jr., *Ius commune, Canon Law, and Common Law in England*, 1752 et seq. Vinogradoff is of the opinion that the knowledge of Roman law possessed by Bracton was based on second hand compilations — such as the writings of Azo and Vacarius — rather than on the original texts of Justinian; see P. Vinogradoff, "Les maximes dans l'ancien Droit commun anglais", in his *Collected Papers*, vol. 2 (Oxford, 1928), 241.

[18] See G. Post, "Bracton on Kingship", 42 *Tulane Law Review* 519 et seq. (1968); and B. Tierney, "Bracton on Government", 314, within his collection of writings published under the title of *Church, Law and Constitutional Thought in the Middle Ages* (London, 1979). The original numeration of the pages of each article has been kept in that collection.

civil law[19]. The same can be even said about certain aspects of criminal law[20] and judicial organization. With regard to the latter, it seems that he borrowed from canon law the distinction between ordinary and delegate judges[21], and — as Glanvill had done before him — the rules concerning the rejection of jurors[22].

However, the precise measure of Roman-canonical inspiration which was present in the work of Bracton has a relative significance for purposes of this essay. Although Maitland described the treatise as "the crown and flower of English medieval jurisprudence"[23], it is doubtful how far Bracton's work reflected actual judicial practice of his time. Plucknett declares that Bracton's aim lay rather in correcting the numerous errors which he saw in common law. Consequently it would be a mistake to consider the treatise an accurate source of knowledge about English law of the time[24]. Similar conclusions have been reached more recently by some other historians of law, who minimize the actual connection that Bracton's treatise had with real juridical life[25].

---

[19] The term "civil law" is used here with its continental meaning: *droit civil.*

[20] Scrutton has written in this regard: "On some points, e.g. that in the case of those engaged at or helping in a fight, the blow of one is the blow of all, the law estated by Bracton is still the law of England, and this rule is directly derived from the Canon law, which follows the Digest" (T. E. Scrutton, *The Influence of the Roman Law*, 108).

[21] Ibid., 106

[22] See H.D. Hazeltine, *Roman and Canon Law*, 758 et seq.; and T.F.T. Plucknett, *A Concise History*, 128 et seq.

[23] F. Pollock / F.W. Maitland, *The History of English Law*, vol. 1, 206.

[24] T.F.T. Plucknett, "The Relations between Roman Law and English Common Law down to the Sixteenth Century: A General Survey", 3 *The University of Toronto Law Journal* 37 et seq. (1939).

[25] See J.H. Baker, introduction to *The Reports of Sir John Spelman*,33 et seq., and S.F.C. Milsom, *Historical Foundations*, 41 et seq. Baker, however,

Certainly Bracton sought to understand and explain English law from the perspective of the general legal theory of his age. This entailed making use of the system developed by canonists and civilians, which seemed to furnish the only adequate tools with which to organize the then chaotic picture of common law[26]. It would not be surprising if, in that effort, the daily reality of English juridical life should have been misrepresented. This, in turn, might have caused Bracton's work to be rejected by a judicature jealous of its originality and autonomy, and itself still in the midst of being fully developed.

However, even if we assume the foregoing to be absolutely correct, it would not be accurate to conclude that, in terms of effect on the evolution of English law, Bracton's work was stillborn. At most, we could say that it went into a long hibernation. Indeed, the revival of Bracton's ideas by virtue of Coke's extensive use of his work in the sixteenth century is well known[27], and it is difficult to name an author more influential than Coke was on the jurisprudence of the common law. Commenting on this, Yale has stressed that Coke did not resort to Bracton because he had the intention of importing foreign legal doctrines; rather it happened because the common lawyers were beginning to think in terms of substantive law[28] — exactly what Bracton had done in his attempt to modify the course of common law, imprisoned as it then was in the spider's web of procedural machinery.

We shall now turn to the second period under analysis here: the sixteenth century. During this time concepts taken from Roman law

---

notes that Bracton was utilized as a source by the common law courts from the times of Henry VII.

[26] See P. Stein, *The Character and Influence of the Roman Civil Law*, 152 et seq.

[27] See T.E. Scrutton, *The Influence of the Roman Law*, 129 et seq.

[28] D.E.C. Yale, "Of no Mean Authority: Some Later Uses of Bracton", in *On the Laws and Customs of England. Essays in Honor of Samuel E. Thorne* (Chapel Hill, 1981), 383 et seq. Yale adds, however, that the influence of Bracton was eclipsed, in the eighteenth century, by the works of Blackstone.

had a receptive audience in Britain, as it tended to be identified with certain points of view regarding the monarchy which appealed to the Tudor monarchs. Specific manifestations of that receptive atmosphere were the creation of civil law chairs by Henry VIII in Oxford and Cambridge, and the grouping of English civilians together in a guild called "Doctor's Commons"[29].

From our standpoint, the central figure during that period was Christopher Saint German, already discussed in the context of the canonical influence in the Court of Chancery[30]. While it is not necessary to repeat observations made in regard to the connection between *Doctor and Student* and the canonical and theological thinking of the time, there are two points which are worth stressing in the present context.

First, when trying to establish Chancery's role in English legal system, St. German declares a preference for the canonical notion of *æquitas* over the Aristotelian concept of *epikeia*. The latter would permit the judge only to recognize exceptions to the application of a general norm. For him, however, the idea of equity also possesses a positive meaning: it makes it possible to enforce the duties of conscience and thereby protect rights conferred by natural law, even if they are not be protected by human law[31].

Second, and derived from the first point, St. German's contractual theories related to the Chancery appear to have been strongly influenced by Christian and canonical doctrine, especially in relation

---

[29] See T.F.T. Plucknett, *The Relations between Roman Law and English Common Law*, 46 et seq.; M. Sarfatti, "Influenza reciproca del diritto romano e del diritto anglosassone", in *Studi in memoria di Aldo Albertoni*, vol. 3 (Padova, 1983), 570 et seq.

[30] In addition to the bibliography there cited, some suggestive remarks on St. German, in the context of the sixteenth century English civilians, have been written by D.R. Coquillette, *The Civilian Writers of Doctor's Commons, London* (Berlin 1988), 48 et seq.

[31] See J.L. Barton's introduction to the Selden Society edition of *Doctor and Student*, xlvii et seq.

to the possibility of requiring specific performance of informal contracts in cases when *animus se obligandi* exists[32].

Together with the author of the *Doctor and Student*, other civilians, generally linked to Doctor's Commons, carried out functions of importance in the legal, political, and cultural life of sixteenth century England: among them were Thomas Legge, Thomas Smith, Alberico Gentili, William Fulbecke and John Cowell[33]. It is true that those jurists — perhaps with the exception of Fulbecke — belonged in continental *ius civile* circles rather than in the sphere of *ius canonicum* (although the two were hardly separable within the *ius commune*). It is also true that it has not been proven thus far that their work had direct repercussion on specific points of English law. However, it cannot be denied that the methodological enrichment they brought to English jurisprudence contributed in some way to instilling an open-minded spirit towards the reception of continental ideas among common lawyers[34].

Ideas drawn from the *ius commune* had yet another channel of entry into the British Isles: legal maxims. They were in use from the twelfth century, and their popularity amongst English jurists continued until late in the nineteenth century.

---

[32] See ibid., lv et seq. See also W.S. Holdsworth, *The Early History of Equity*, 297 et seq.; A.W.B. Simpson, *A History of the Common Law of Contract*, 376 et seq.; and P. Vinogradoff, *Reason and Conscience*, 199 et seq.

[33] See D.R. Coquillette, *The Civilian Writers of Doctor's Commons*, 44 et seq.; B.P. Levack, *The Civil Lawyers in England 1603-1641: A Political Study* (Oxford, 1973); G.D. Squibb, *Doctor's Commons* (Oxford, 1977); P. Stein, *The Character and Influence of the Roman Civil Law*, 186 et seq.

[34] Coquillette has emphasized that those civilians made notable methodological contributions to English law, notwithstanding their scant direct influence on the practical development of common law. Above all, they were the pioneers of comparative law in Great Britain, and their use of comparative method made possible an important flow of critical elements that advanced subsequent improvements of English law (D.R. Coquillette, *The Civilian Writers of Doctor's Commons*, 94-96).

In the Anglo-American legal world, maxims have traditionally enjoyed undisputed authority, often being quoted in judicial sentences as basis for the decision[35]. In *Doctor and Student* they are included among the foundations for the law of the kingdom, granting them an almost absolute incontestability, as they constitute expressions of the law of reason[36]. Coke refers to them in the following words: "maxima est eius dignitas et certissima auctoritas"[37].

No doubt Maitland was exaggerating when he affirmed that, between the thirteenth and nineteenth century, any English jurist employing a Latin maxim was quoting the *Liber Sextus* although he might not have been conscious of it[38]. To prove the point, it is sufficient to look at the book of common law maxims compiled by Sir Francis Bacon, perhaps the most famous of the works of that genre produced in England. Although written in Latin, the majority of maxims come neither from the *Sextus* nor from Roman sources, although the author does use the latter to demonstrate the meaning of the maxims he conveys[39]. However, what in any event can be affirmed is that, from the beginnings of the common law, the *regulæ iuris* of the *Liber Sextus*, together with other Roman texts — mainly the *Digest* — provided one of the resources of choice among English writers and judges[40]. Through them, important aspects of Roman-

---

[35] With regard to the maxims in Anglo-American law, see the writings of Pound, Stein, Vinogradoff and Williams cited in note 89 of this chapter.

[36] See chapter 8, pages 56-58 of the Selden Society edition.

[37] Quoted by J. Williams, *Latin Maxims in English Law*, vol. 1, 284.

[38] F. Pollock / F.W. Maitland, *The History of English Law*, vol. 1, 218.

[39] Bacon's book was published posthumously, in 1630, and it is usually known by the abridged title *Collection Of Some Principal Rvles and Maximes of the Common Lawes of England*. A photostat reprint was realized in Amsterdam in 1969.

[40] One of the best known examples is the commentary on the *regulæ iuris* of the *Digest* written by Sir Thomas Eden in 1633. Unlike Bacon, however, Eden did not try to connect the Roman rules to the context of British law: he limited himself to explaining their meaning according to the civilian tradition.

canonical jurisprudence were assimilated by the Anglo-American legal tradition[41].

[41] With regard to the role played by the maxims of equity — some of them presumably of canonical origin, as I said before — on the development of the North American equity, see the interesting remarks written by Roscoe Pound, *On Certain Maxims of Equity*, 259 et seq.

Part III

The Influence of Canon Law on the Different Areas of English Law

Chapter 6

Marriage and Family

1. English Matrimonial Law

If there is one area of western law where the influence of the canon law is unquestionable, it is marriage law, and through it a significant part of family law. This influence may be evaluated from very different points of view, but in spite of the profound uncertainties and transformation western law is currently undergoing[1], our cultural environment retains the essential configuration of marriage based on Judæo-Christian moral values which — especially from the twelfth to the sixteenth centuries — were legally articulated by the law of the Catholic Church[2].

---

[1] See in this regard the suggestive essay by M.A. Glendon, *The Transformation of Family Law. State, Law and Family in the United States and Western Europe* (Chicago, 1989).

[2] See an excellent exposition on the evolution of the canon law on marriage in the extensive article by G. Le Bras, "La doctrine du mariage chez les théologiens et les canonistes depuis l'an mille", under the entry *mariage* in

The reason for the vast influence of the canon law is the dominance exercised by ecclesiastical power by means of that branch of law throughout the Middle Ages and, in many countries, well into the Modern period. Jurisdiction over matrimonial causes in Europe became the almost exclusive territory of ecclesiastical courts, from at least the eleventh century[3]. The Church was able to assert its jurisdiction based on a distinctive notion of marriage, considered as a sacrament and a contract at once. Catholic theology and the canon law claimed that, marriage being a sacrament, control of the union between baptized persons must rest within the competence of the spiritual power; and, since the sacrament was inseparable from the legal contract, that competence was not only moral but also of a jurisdictional character.

For a long period, that interpretation was accepted by the secular power. This is not surprising if we consider it in the context of a strong pontificate and a society which, from a religious standpoint, was substantially monolithic. The situation began to change with Luther's novel ideas on marriage and the Church, and with the reception of these ideas in the kingdoms accepting the Reformation. By that time, however, there was already a complete and established legal doctrine on marriage, constructed by papal decretals and the writings of medieval canonists. So profound was the mark left by that doctrine on European culture and customs that it remained within the legislation of those countries where marriage gradually became primarily a civil institution.

---

the *Dictionnaire de Théologie Catholique*, vol. 9 (Paris, 1926), 2123-2317. For development of the juridical concept and the regulation of marriage in the western world, see J. Gaudemet, *Le mariage en Occident. Les moeurs et le droit* (Paris, 1987).

[3] The history of the ecclesiastical jurisdiction in the Occident is well explained by A. Esmein, *Le mariage en Droit canonique* (Paris, 2d ed, 1929), 1-66. The Church jurisdiction took the validity of marriage as its central concern, but in practice extended far beyond and judged issues like conjugal separation, financial relations between the spouses, legitimacy of offspring, etc. In these latter aspects, however, the activity of the Church's jurisdiction was not equally intense throughout; in France, for example, there was a degree of concurrence with secular jurisdiction in causes concerning marital property and legitimacy.

Hence Esmein has written, with regard to the institution of civil marriage in Protestant nations: "it was like a branch detached from the trunk and planted in new ground"[4].

In England, the strength of canonical influence was even greater. Leaving aside the situation prior to the Norman Conquest, it is clear that William the Conqueror's separation of jurisdictional fields was the milestone that made possible the definitive appropriation of jurisdiction over marriage by ecclesiastical courts. Furthermore, that exclusive jurisdiction was destined to last much longer in England than in other European nations[5].

On the Continent the process of secularization of marriage began in the sixteenth century with the Protestant reform, and continued without interruption, impelled first by regalism and later by rationalism and legal positivism. Instead in the English kingdom, if we except the ephemeral establishment of civil marriage by Cromwell[6], matrimony was retained within the religious sphere until the nineteenth century. Only in 1857 did the Matrimonial Causes Act transfer to a new court — the Court for Divorce and Matrimonial Causes — the jurisdiction previously exercised by ecclesiastical courts[7].

In theory, the jurisdiction of the ecclesiastical courts was limited to matters referring to the marital relationship itself, while common law courts had jurisdiction over the issues concerning the property of the

---

[4] "Ce fut comme un rameau détaché du tronc et planté dans une terre nouvelle". Ibid., 34.

[5] Already in Glanvill's treatise it is pointed out that the validity of marriage can only be determined by the ecclesiastical jurisdiction (see J. Jackson, *The Formation and Annulment of Marriage* (London, 1951), 7.

[6] See E. Stocquart, "Le mariage civil en Angleterre sous Cromwell et son institution dans le Nouveau-Monde en 1665", *Revue de l'Université de Bruxelles* 441 et seq. (1909).

[7] The fact that marriage was a religious matter in England did not mean that only marriage in the Anglican Church was recognized; in the eighteenth century, the ecclesiastical courts admitted the validity of the marriage of Jews and Quakers (J.H. Baker, *An Introduction to English Legal History*, 391).

spouses. However, in reality the intervention of ecclesiastical courts was much broader. More often than not, unless the ownership of land was at stake, the Church courts determined property issues, as well as issues involving legitimacy and guardianship of children. The jurisdiction of ecclesiastical courts even extended, through the use of criminal remedies, to the repression of certain unlawful activities with only a collateral connection with matrimony.

Through the jurisdiction of ecclesiastical courts, canon law contributed — to England and to the rest of Europe — a legal construct of marriage, rooted in the theological doctrine elaborated by medieval scholasticism, and founded both on the Sacred Scriptures and the patristic writings of the first centuries of Christianity[8]. It asserted that matrimony was a primarily consensual contract, to some extent of public character, subject to a certain form of celebration (mandatory *ad validitatem* after the Council of Trent), objectively directed at procreation, and with an intrinsic tendency toward the stability of the bond and the conjugal society. Around these coordinates, courts progressively built a system setting forth the conditions for the validity of the contract and establishing the causes of nullity, dissolution or separation of matrimony. These legal principles, moreover, would later influence central conceptions of western legal culture in the law of contracts, in matters relating to, for example, freedom of consent, error or fraud[9].

This concept of matrimony gradually permeated English legal life, through the work of ecclesiastical courts over the space of nearly eight centuries of undisputed jurisdiction in the matter. As Helmholz has expressively noted, during that extended period the canon law of

---

[8] In relation to the scriptural, patristic and theological foundation of the notion of matrimony in canon law, see the volumes which, under the title of *El matrimonio, misterio y signo*, have been published by the University of Navarra; especially interesting are the first volume (covering from the first century until Saint Augustine, edited by E. Saldón) and the third (from the ninth to the thirteenth centuries, edited by T. Rincón); both were published in Pamplona, 1971.

[9] H.J. Berman, *Law and Revolution*, 226 et seq.

marriage was also the law of England[10]. It was not a foreign law that imposed itself with greater or lesser force, and for a more or less prolonged period. It was rather an integral part — and an important one — of English law. This assertion may seem excessive to minds accustomed to the categories of legal positivism, yet it fits well the historical context of a system accustomed to recognizing the existence of other normative bodies of law, independent and complementary to the common law of the kingdom[11].

Certainly, the ecclesiastical ideas on marriage were to some extent a novelty and they were not easily accepted by English society. While ecclesiastical matrimonial jurisdiction gained control quite rapidly, control was not sufficient. The real issue was changing the very concept of matrimony within the population, substituting for the pre-Christian vision, which considered it a private union not necessarily indissoluble, a new concept which understood matrimony as a binding legal contract, whose essential traits were set forth by public norms of *ius cogens*, and which was inescapably subject to judicial power. This task was achieved slowly, in a process that may be considered complete by the late fifteenth century[12].

---

[10] R.H. Helmholz, *Marriage Litigation in Medieval England*, 3.

[11] In similar circumstances were both the equity administered in Chancery, as we have seen in chapter 4, and the law merchant. These branches of English law possessed their own jurisdiction, which they maintained until the late nineteenth century.

[12] Helmholz has called attention to this fact after an extensive and careful research on matrimonial causes before the ecclesiastical courts in medieval England. He observed that most lawsuits were directed not at declarations of nullity but at the declaration of existence of a marriage, and consequently they were aimed at having the other party constrained to admit and fulfil the contract. These data seem surprising when compared with what has been common practice in the ecclesiastical jurisdiction in recent centuries. Trying to find an explanation, Helmholz concludes that, naturally, one of the reasons was the absence of a determined form of marriage as a condition of validity. However in his opinion — which I share — the main reason was the resistance of the ancient conception of marriage as a private contract — often not respected — which would only gradually give way to the publicist

In the long run, however, the canonical concept prevailed, both in the British Isles and on the Continent. And it influenced western thought so deeply that it was able to resist even the push of post-revolutionary secularizing currents in the nineteenth century. What happened at that time was that the State apparatus replaced the ecclesiastical judicial institutions as an enforcement authority, although it is true that, by changing the ideological tenets which had sustained the concept, the possibility of dissolving a marriage was accentuated[13].

The process by which classical canon law was assimilated by English ecclesiastical courts, and subsequently integrated into the civil regulation of matrimony in Anglo-American countries, is sufficiently well-known so not to require further explanation here.

It occurred, moreover, in a manner similar to that of western legal systems. No doubt the action of English ecclesiastical jurisdiction during the Middle Ages reveals some peculiarities, above all in the procedural domain, vis-à-vis the theoretical model developed by canonists and the Papacy. Yet many of these deviations can be explained in terms of judicial efficiency, as the Church courts sought to adapt their judicial practices to the necessities of life[14]. In essence

---

perspective of matrimony proper to canon law. This situation does not appear to have been exclusive to England, but rather quite extended throughout Europe. Furthermore — Helmholz adds — the council of Trent could establish a determined public form of celebrating marriage in the sixteenth century because the social mentality had experienced a progressive change in relation to the previous centuries. Helmholz's conclusions certainly correspond with the data found in the ecclesiastical records, which reveal that the claims concerning the validity of marriage declined considerably in the fifteenth century, while the claims of nullity increased. See R.H. Helmholz, *Marriage Litigation in Medieval England*, 72 et seq. and 167 et seq.

[13] Nevertheless, the extension and flexibility of divorce in most western countries nowadays, together with the emerging concept of extra-marital family, seem to announce a certain return to the private notion of marriage, and even to the Roman idea of marriage as a mere factual union with legal effects.

[14] R.H. Helmholz, *Marriage Litigation in Medieval England*, 112 et seq. One of the more picturesque peculiarities was probably the unorthodox means

English ecclesiastical courts applied Roman canon law — the canon law that was common to the whole of Christendom, of which England was fully a part.

The dependence on the canon law of Rome survived Henry VIII's schism. The Crown preserved the ecclesiastical courts' jurisdiction over matrimonial causes, and canonical norms were scarcely modified, either from a substantive or a procedural perspective[15]. Even the issue of divorce always remained outside the jurisdictional domain of English ecclesiastical courts — it could only be granted through an Act of

---

of proof of the impediment of impotence that the courts of certain English Dioceses sometimes utilized, consisting in the inspection of the man by a group of "honest women".

It is worth transcribing the description of one of such cases contained in a document of 1433 from the archive of the Diocese of York: "Ipsa iurata ostendebat mammillas suas denudatas ac manibus suis ad dictam ignem calefactis virgam et testiculos dicti Johanis palpavit et tenuit ac eundem Johannem amplexabatur et sæpius osculabatur ad eundem Johannem ostendendum virilitatem et potentiam suam in quantum potuit excitavit, precipiendo sibi quod pro pudore tunc ibidem probaret et redderet se virum. Et dicit examinata et diligenter requisita quod toto tempore supradicto predicta virga fix fuit longitudinis trium pollicium..., absque incremento vel decremento aliquali permanens". Once the "inspection" had ended — the report continues — "mulieres, ut dicit, tunc una voce maledicebant eo quod ipse presumeret ducere in uxorem aliquam iuvenem mulierem ipsam defraudando nisi potuisset eidem melius deservire et placere".

The procedure, however, not always produced negative results. In another document of the same period, also from York, one of the "examiners" testifies that "virga predicti Willelmi fuit melioris quantitatis in longitudine et grossitudine quam virga ipsius mariti uncquam fuit". The quotations are taken from R.H. Helmholz, *Marriage Litigation*, 89).

[15] See M. Ingram, *Church Courts, Sex and Marriage in England, 1570-1640* (Cambridge, 1990), 41 et seq.; E.J. Carlson, *Marriage and the English Reformation* (Cambridge, Mass., 1994); R.H. Helmholz, *The Spirit of Classical Canon Law*, 229.

Parliament[16]. It was not until 1857 that it became possible to break the conjugal bond through judicial channels, and then not before the Church courts, but before the recently created Court for Divorce and Matrimonial Causes[17].

It is interesting to note that the reformed English Church not merely safeguarded existing canon law, but seems to have incorporated subsequent changes in Roman canon law. A legal attraction toward continental canon law may be observed in the rules concerning celebration of marriages. By the time the Council of Trent required a certain form for the validity of the matrimony (1563), the *Tametsi* decree no longer had any binding force in Great Britain. Even so, English ecclesiastical courts followed the Trent guidelines to the extent feasible, in particular trying to enforce the celebration *in facie Ecclesiæ* of marriages previously contracted in an irregular manner. In 1753, this sentiment moved Parliament to enact a law requiring that, to be valid, every marriage had to take place in a church before the presence of a duly ordained minister[18].

---

[16] The position of the Anglican Church in regard to divorce has been studied by A. Winnett, *Marriage an Remarriage in Anglicanism* (London, 1961) and *The Church and Divorce* (London, 1973); and also by F. Ramos Bossini, *La indisolubilidad matrimonial en el derecho anglicano* (Granada, 1977).

[17] See J. Bryce, "Marriage and Divorce under Roman and English Law", in *Select Essays in Anglo-American Legal History*", vol. 3, 822 et seq. The intervention of ecclesiastical courts was restricted to dictating the sentence of separation *a mensa et thoro* (of table and bed) required — since 1798 — to begin the proceedings of divorce in the House of Lords. Bryce notes that divorce was utilized mainly by men: until 1801 no woman obtained a divorce from Parliament (Ibid., 824).

[18] Ibid., 814 et seq.

2. Ecclesiastical Jurisdiction in Matters Related to Matrimony

At the beginning of this chapter, I mentioned that ecclesiastical jurisdiction went beyond the strict confines of relationship between the persons which is the essence of matrimony. Indeed the Church courts always applied an expansionist reading of their jurisdiction, seeking to reach other areas of legal life that had a more or less direct connection with the marital relationship. While their success was not complete, they managed to broaden their jurisdictional sphere to quite a few matters, most of which would be part of what we today call family law.

In the area of marital property it is clear that the canonical solemnization of a matrimony had a direct influence on the applicable common law rules relating to dower, dowry and *maritagium*. In the case of dower (the husband's donation to the wife at the church door, on their wedding day), royal courts only recognized claims to dower for marriages celebrated *in facie Ecclesiæ*, denying the protection to dower granted in the course of a clandestine marriage[19]. On the other hand, Glanvill stated as a rule of common law the principle that the adulterous wife who was separated from her husband forfeited her dowry (i.e. the wife's donation to the husband upon marriage); this rule followed the guidelines established in papal decretals, and was later confirmed by the second statute of Westminster in 1285[20]. With regard to the rules governing *maritagium* (the father's donation to the daughter on the occasion of matrimony), Glanvill again provided an interesting insight: the pledge of faith made in the context of a canonical marriage was the basis upon which Church courts later relied to exercise jurisdiction in

---

[19] See J.H. Baker, *An Introduction to English Legal History*, 229; T.F.T. Plucknett, *A Concise History*, 566.

[20] J.A. Brundage, *Law, Sex, and Christian Society in Medieval Europe* (Chicago, 1987), 408; F. Pollock / F.W. Maitland, *History of English Law*, vol. 2, 394 et seq.; M.M. Sheehan, "The Influence of Canon Law on the Property Rights of Married Women in England", 25 *Medieval Studies* 110, 115 (1963).

order to protect the spouses in the event that the donor or his successors did not perform their part of the bargain[21].

The division of goods in case of matrimonial nullity or separation was another area where canon law claimed jurisdiction, based on a number of decretals, some of them addressed to English subjects. It is unclear to what extent this jurisdiction was actually exercised in medieval England. However, according to Sheehan, Church courts unquestionably possessed jurisdiction over some issues related to the portion of real estate on the dowry. And, although their activity was likely much broader, it is at least certain that bishops exerted an important moral pressure in defense of the property rights of married women in those cases where marriages had been dissolved or a couple separated[22].

The protection of the rights of married women that the Church provided in England had two other expressions. First, an effort by the ecclesiastical authorities to seek acceptance of the wife's right to leave a will, which was probably influenced by the hope that she might make bequests in alms. In various periods, common law courts categorically rejected this right. In spite of it, there is documentary evidence from the thirteenth and fourteenth centuries revealing that, in practice, many women wrote out testaments and these were effectively observed[23]. The second expression is the interest shown by the Church in assuring the rights of every widow: namely her freedom to choose her status (whether or not to remarry, and if so, with whom), and her right to a share of her deceased husband's goods. This freedom of choice was accepted and eventually reflected by the provisions of the *Magna Carta*.

---

[21] See S.F.C. Milsom, *Historical Foundations*, 202; T.F.T. Plucknett, *A Concise History*, 547 et seq. It has not been investigated yet to what extent the ecclesiastical courts actually intervened in those issues.

[22] M.M. Sheehan, *The Influence of Canon Law on the Property Rights of Married Women*, 115 et seq.

[23] F. Pollock / F.W. Maitland, *History of English Law*, vol. 2, 428 et seq.; M.M. Sheehan, *The Influence of Canon Law on the Property Rights of Married Women*, 118 et seq.

In the field of inheritance, however, the common law came to reject the Church's claims; the widow's right to a portion of the belongings of her dead husband would only be enforced in case of succession[24].

Beyond the administration of marital property, the Church courts also sought to extend their jurisdiction to issues relating to the offspring, particularly issues concerning legitimacy and legitimation, where medieval canon law had developed a series of norms. Their record here was mixed. With regard to the latter, English bishops suffered a clear defeat when, in the Statute of Merton of 1236, the English nobility refused to accept legitimation of children by the subsequent marriage of their parents (*nolumus leges Angliæ mutari*). This step would have entailed modifying the traditional rules of hereditary succession and adopting instead the canonical doctrine[25]. On the other hand, the legitimacy of offspring born of a putative marriage was accepted by the common law, at least for some time[26]. And in any event the Church courts retained jurisdiction over the issue of bastardy through the nineteenth century, so that the common law courts often

[24] M.M. Sheehan, *The Influence of Canon Law on the Property Rights of Married Women*, 116 et seq., 122 et seq.; see also, from the same author, "Canon Law and English Institutions: Some Notes on Current Research", in *Proceedings of the Second International Congress of Medieval Canon Law* (E Civitate Vaticana, 1965), 394 et seq.

[25] See F.W. Maitland, *Roman Canon Law in the Church of England*, 52 et seq. Legitimation by subsequent marriage was not admitted by English law until the Legitimacy Act of 1926. In the United States this rule became accepted earlier, as it did not have the same consequences as in England with regard to hereditary issues (H. Milton Colvin, "Roman and Civil Elements in Sources of the Law of the United States", in *Studi in memoria di Aldo Albertoni*, vol. 3 (Padova, 1938), 147.

[26] However, from the fourteenth century on the common lawyers abandoned this canonical doctrine. They began to disregard the good or bad faith of the parents in relation to the nullity of their marriage, and to adopt instead the view that legitimacy depended on whether the spouses had in life contested the validity of their union (F. Pollock / F.W. Maitland, *History of English Law*, vol. 2, 375 et seq.).

had to remit the question to ecclesiastical jurisdiction when it became an issue at trial[27].

Furthermore, during the Later Middle Ages ecclesiastical courts devoted significant time and resources to obtaining support for illegitimate children from their natural father, avoiding the common law tendency to leave them unprotected as *filii nullius*. The method for securing such support was often conciliation, but the Church courts also resorted to penal remedies, including excommunication. Thus, when the Elizabethan Poor Law in 1576, granted to justices of the peace authority to demand child support from fathers of illegitimate offspring, it did not actually introduce a new legal concept in England, but merely provided a new mechanism to enforce an existing obligation that had hitherto been within the realm of ecclesiastical jurisdiction (whose coercive power in this area may have decreased by this time)[28].

Ecclesiastical courts also extended their jurisdiction to the guardianship of minors, particularly during the fourteenth and fifteenth centuries, filling the void left by the common law in this field[29]. The Church's traditional interest in the protection of *miserabiles personæ* and its intervention in matrimonial causes of every kind certainly made

---

[27] R.H. Helmholz, "Bastardy Litigation in Medieval England", in his collection of articles published under the title of *Canon Law and the Law of England*, 187 et seq. Helmholz affirms that, in the conflicts between royal and ecclesiastical courts in issues related to bastardy, the common lawyers remained inflexible only when principles of hereditary succession to land were at stake.

[28] Although Elizabethan law possessed some original traits, many of its characteristics corresponded to the previous ecclesiastical practice: e.g. a summary procedure to determine paternity, and the possibility of issuing immediate judicial orders to provide for the support of offspring. This subject has been accurately studied by R.H. Helmholz, "Support Orders, Church Courts, and the Rule of *filius nullius*": A Reassessment of the Common Law", in *Common law and the law of England*, 169 et seq.

[29] As Maitland wrote, "no part of our old law was more disjointed and incomplete than that which deals with guardianship of infants" (F. Pollock / F.W. Maitland, *History of English Law*, vol. 2, 443).

it easier for the Church to assert jurisdiction in this area. However, it was the ecclesiastical jurisdiction on testamentary subjects which served as the basis for the Church's foray into guardianship[30]. Canon law did not have its own specific regulations governing the matter. Therefore, the Church courts applied the Roman rules of *cura* and *tutela* to regulate the appointment and fix the obligations of guardians.

For the rest, ecclesiastical influence on this area does not seem to have been limited to temporarily filling an existing void. By virtue of their early intervention in this area, the ecclesiastical courts assisted in the assimilation of romanistic concepts in the English law of guardianship. Indeed, prominent scholars have remarked on the similarities between the jurisdiction of the Roman *prætor* over minors, and that exercised by Chancery over infants during the fifteenth and sixteenth centuries[31]. It has also been pointed out that, in the seventeenth century, English law reversed the previous status quo and adopted the Roman law's provision permitting the father to determine the custody of his offspring by testamentary disposition[32].

Outside the immediate domain of family law, as a consequence of the manifold ecclesiastical jurisdiction over matrimonial matters, the Church would extend its reach even into the criminal law. It was then

---

[30] See R.H. Helmholz, "The Roman Law of Guardianship in England, 1300-1600", *in Canon Law and the Law of England*, 211-245; and more recently, by the same author, "The English Law of Wills and the *ius commune*, 1450-1640", in L. Bonfield, ed, *Marriage, Property, and Succession* (Berlin, 1992), 318 et seq.

[31] T.E. Scrutton, *The Influence of the Roman Law*, 158 et seq.; G. Spence, *Equitable Jurisdiction*, vol. 1, 605 et seq.

[32] R.H. Helmholz , *The Roman Law of Guardianship*, 244. Some historians have been reticent to admit that these analogies between English legislation and the Roman law norms applied by ecclesiastical courts may be the sign of a canonical influence on the common law. In this regard Helmholz has expressively written: "to exclude the possibility that the influence of Roman law principles came through the Courts of the Church seems as incautious as to adopt the idea automatically once the similarities are noted" (Ibid., 245).

accepted that nearly all matters concerning sexual morality were connected with marriage, and consequently that they were the business of ecclesiastical authorities. The natural effect was that many moral offences became legally punishable. Thus, throughout the Middle Ages, fornication, adultery, incest and bigamy were treated as crimes, and their repression was assumed by the spiritual rather than the secular power (and it is interesting to note that this resulted in some mitigation of prior customs[33]). English ecclesiastical courts punished these crimes in diverse manners: sometimes through corporal punishment, frequently through pecuniary sanctions, and on occasions even using marriage as a form of remedy.

The latter occurred with the so-called *abjuratio sub pœna nubendi*, which fell into disuse in the fourteenth century, and which constituted one of the clearest deviations from canonical models contained in the decretal law[34]. In brief, its goal was to force individuals convicted of fornication to abstain from future illicit sexual relations. To accomplish this, a man and a woman were sometimes forced to marry conditionally, by means of a formula like the following: "Hic accipio te in uxorem meam [in virum meum] si ex nunc cognoscam te [cognoscas me] carnaliter" ("I accept you as my wife [my husband] if from now on we have carnal knowledge"). If sexual relations occurred again, the condition would be fulfilled and the spouses would be automatically joined by canonical matrimony. Through this practice, the Church either avoided a relapse of the crime or regularized the situation, at least in theory.

---

[33] Maitland points out that ecclesiastical courts sanctioned such offences with punishments that were less cruel than those which would have been imposed by the temporal power: among the Germanic and Anglo-Saxon peoples, such conducts were sometimes penalized with mutilation — castration and blinding, principally — or even death. F. Pollock / F.W. Maitland, *History of English Law*, vol. 2, 543 et seq.

[34] See R.H. Helmholz, "Abjuration *sub pœna nubendi* in the Church Courts of Medieval England", in *Canon law and the law of England*, 145 et seq. The event of the progressive disappearance of the *abjuratio*, on the other hand, illustrates the tendency of English ecclesiastical courts to make their practice conform to the guidelines of the canon law.

The preceding pages sufficiently illustrate the following historical evidence: that, for a considerable period of time, English marriage law, and also — to some extent — family law, was the law administered by canonical institutions. It is true that many of the ecclesiastical solutions only made sense within the framework of a feudal society and, therefore, died with the end of the Middle Ages. However, this is also true of many solutions adopted by the common law (especially in the area of real property). Yet no one disputes that they are an integral part of the history of Anglo-American law, or that they have contributed to moulding its current form.

It cannot be emphasized too strongly that, despite the profound changes undergone by western mores related to marriage, the influence of canonical constructs and concepts remains in many areas of the Anglo-American legal tradition (as well as the civil law tradition). It is worth recalling that the Anglo-American concept of "common law marriage" is — in Berman's opinion — a residue of the canon law on marriage as it existed before the Council of Trent[35]. And, according to Brundage, in the legislation of some North-American states some remains of medieval canonical doctrine can be found: e.g. the inspiration of various aspects of divorce taken from canonical ideas about nullity, the survival of the consensual theory of marriage, the "spousal exception" in the law of rape[36], and the repression of prostitution and sodomy[37].

---

[35] See H.J. Berman, *Law and Revolution*, 227. The expression "common law marriage" refers to a *de facto* marriage: i.e. a personal relationship between man and woman where it is considered that a matrimonial intention exists, but where marriage has not been celebrated according to the form required by positive law. In some North American states this relationship is protected in a manner similar to the marriage contracted in legal form (i.e. courts habitually consider them as valid marriages, unless the law of the state declare them expressly void). In England, "common law marriages" were deemed valid until 1753, and in Scotland, until 1940; see S.M. Cretney, *Elements of Family Law* (London, 1987), and A.L. Stroup, *Marriage and Family: A Developmental Approach* (New York, 1966).

From today's point of view, one may well conclude that the survival of some of these elements requires a negative assessment. Yet they cannot be ignored. They are also to some extent counterbalanced by the fact that the solutions adopted by the ecclesiastical jurisdiction were in many areas notably more advanced that those embraced by English common law. The Church courts often took positions which the common law would only adopt much later. Some examples of this have been noted in this chapter: the legitimation of offspring through subsequent marriage, the married woman's freedom to leave a will, and the obligation to provide child support for natural offspring.

---

[36] It means that a violent threat to consummate a sexual act is not punishable when it takes place between persons linked by legitimate matrimony.

[37] See J.A. Brundage, *Law, Sex, and Christian Society*, 611 et seq. Brundage is right in tracing the analogies between the current North American law and the medieval canonical concepts, but in my opinion he is not equally accurate in establishing the causal nexus between them. For example, it is difficult to accept that the consensual theory of marriage arrived in the United States through the hands of Roman canon law, which substantially modified its position in this regard in the council of Trent (*Tametsi* decree, 1563). Rather, it appears to originate in Protestant England, as the Anglican Church, after its detachment from Rome, did not follow the evolution of Roman canon law on that subject. A similar remark could be made in relation to the previously cited affirmation of Berman on the historical links between common law marriage and medieval canon law.

Chapter 7

The Law of Succession

Roscoe Pound once stated that, whereas in civil law systems the core concept is the notion of *will*, in early common law the feudal notion of *relation* between persons provided the main source of juridical rights and obligations[1]. The accuracy of his statement is readily verified in the evolution of English law of succession.

In early English law, succession of real property was the exclusive realm of the common law. As such it was subject to fixed rules that were inherent in feudal society[2]. In principle, the tenant had no say in who would inherit his lands upon his death. The heir was designated automatically, based on his relation to the decedent. One could say that there was no testamentary freedom in relation to real property (although the rigidity of this norm was subsequently eased through the constitution of uses, the predecessor of the trusts[3]).

---

[1] R. Pound, *The Spirit of the Common Law* (Boston, 1921), 20 et seq.

[2] See J.H. Baker, *An Introduction to English Legal History*, 226 et seq.

[3] See R.H. Helmholz, *The English Law of Wills*, 316 et seq. It is not by chance that the protection of the uses was rejected by the common law courts and instead initially conceded to the ecclesiastical courts, and later to the Court of Chancery, whose Roman-canonical inspiration has already been pointed out in chapter 4.

On the other hand, the reverse was true with regard to personal property. The freedom of the deceased to make a will became the dominant theme. It is precisely here that English law developed its rules and doctrines on testamentary succession. What mattered was the expression of the will of a person with regard to the disposition of his property after his death. The reason of this respect for the will of the deceased is that, for a very long time, the Church courts controlled the transfer of chattel property *post mortem*[4]. In England, much more than on the Continent, the basic principles of the testamentary system arose as a result of the role played in their development by the ecclesiastical courts, which in turn grew out of the *ius commune* sources[5]. In this chapter I will describe the diverse historical factors that contributed to place the *post mortem* transfer of *chattels* under ecclesiastical jurisdiction — a jurisdiction which, in some aspects, survived into the nineteenth century[6].

The deep and extensive influence of canon law on the English law of succession is shown by Henry Swinburne's seventeenth century treatise on testaments and last wills, a book which not only explained the law in force at the time it was written, but also had a decisive impact on the subsequent development of this branch of English law[7]. However, it would be inaccurate and overly simplistic to claim that the evolution of the English testamentary system was due exclusively to the intervention of ecclesiastical courts. They certainly provided the starting point and established the key institutions, but over time much of their jurisdiction was gradually absorbed by the common law courts, which left their own

---

[4] On the other hand — I have already mentioned it, in chapter 3, n. 1 — that fact remarkably contributed to accentuate the differentiation between real property and personal property in English law.

[5] R.H. Helmholz, *The English Law of Wills*, 312 et seq.

[6] Especially the probate jurisdiction, which until 1857 would not be transferred to a royal court: the Court of Probate.

[7] It was published in London, in 1641, under the title *A Briefe Treatise of Testaments and Last Willes*. Since then it has been frequently reprinted, and has been the fundamental treatise on the law of succession in England up until the last century.

imprint on many of the legal constructs they had inherited from the ecclesiastical law[8]. In addition, the Court of Chancery assumed a certain competence over succession. How these three jurisdictions managed to coordinate their roles without apparent conflicts, and the exact manner in which they combined into a unified law in this area, is something that has not yet been completely clarified. Hence, much that is contained in the following pages may need to be fine tuned as further research unveils additional information.

1. The Development of Ecclesiastical Jurisdiction on Succession

From the time before the Conquest the very introduction of the concept of a testament in England has been attributed to the Church. It appears that the concept was unknown to the Germanic peoples. According to pagan customs, the goods of the deceased were customarily divided into three parts: one third for the widow, another third for the offspring, and the remaining third for the decedent's soul. The "soul's part" seems at one time to have been either buried or burnt with the body for use in the after-world. With the advent of Christianity, the "soul's part" would acquire a new significance. Because it was free from claims by the relatives, the Church started recommending that it be given for the support of the clergy or for use in works of charity under ecclesiastical supervision.

From this simple and limited beginning, the ecclesiastical authorities progressively gained competence over the interpretation of last wills. In a parallel evolution, Anglo-Saxon law developed several mechanisms enabling voluntary transfers of belongings to be made that would take full effect at death[9]. However, the Norman settlement would drastically

---

[8] See R.H. Helmholz, *The English Law of Wills*, 323 et seq.

[9] See T.F.T. Plucknett, *Concise History*, 734 et seq.; and M.M. Sheehan, *The Will in Medieval England* (Toronto, 1963), 4 et seq., containing a much more detailed exposition. Sheehan's book is indispensable to understand fully the development of the English law of succession.

modify these practices, especially by eliminating any element of freedom in the transfer of real estate. This rule became central to English law for many centuries[10], but at the same time the distribution and transfer of chattels would, under the guidance of the ecclesiastical institutions, take a quite different route.

It is well-known that medieval canon law paid close attention to succession. This attention can be traced to two main concerns[11]. One was an interest in assuring proper control over the transfer of ecclesiastical property. The other was a desire to ensure the fulfilment of legacies for charitable purposes ("pious causes"). The Church actively encouraged these arrangements for the soul's needs even while administering the last sacraments to a person on his death bed. In fact, the will was not only conceived of as an instrument for religious purposes, but as a religious act in itself[12]. The canonists, especially with regard to gifts in alms, developed a distinctive doctrine, building upon by Roman sources[13], but also embracing important other characteristics[14], such as flexibility in the formalities necessary for the validation of wills[15].

---

[10] There were efforts, from different institutions, aimed at permitting the transfer of land property through *mortis causa* donations, but none of them would succeed. See M.M. Sheehan, *The Will in Medieval England*, 266 et seq.

[11] Ibid., 119 et seq.

[12] Thus the will tended to be headed with references to the Trinity, to the Virgin and the saints, and the provisions relating to the different aspects of the funeral ceremony preceded the provisions of strictly economic content.

[13] See W.W. Buckland / A.D. Mc Nair, *Roman Law and Common Law* (Cambridge, 1965; reprint of the 2d ed), 148 et seq.

[14] See H. Auffroy, *Evolution du testament en France des origines au treizième siècle* (Paris, 1899); J. Hannan, *The Canon Law of Wills* (Washington, D.C., 1934).

[15] One of the reasons for this was obviously the fact that many legacies were carried out on the deathbed, before a clergyman who attended the dying in his last moments. Hence the canon law admitted the validity of verbal

Naturally, the elaboration of the canonical doctrine related to inheritance served the interests of the Church: defence of the freedom of testation may be understood as a defence of the freedom to bequeath property to the Church. This is obviously one reason the Church made an effort to make it the norm in the English kingdom. However, the practical reach of the doctrine went far beyond advancing the interests of the Church. Eventually it inspired all English testamentary law, due to the confluence of a series of historical factors among which the attitude of the common law courts played a central role.

In the context of the separation of jurisdictional spheres decreed by William I, the transfer of property at death was — from the perspective of the time — of a mixed nature. It certainly interested the civil courts, but ecclesiastical jurisdiction was not indifferent to what might come of the property donated by the deceased for charitable purposes — and charity was then a matter which corresponded exclusively to the Church.

The role of the common law progressively centered on inheritance of real property, which the Crown wished to maintain under its control at all costs[16]. In this field, the common law courts developed a set of rules which eliminated the possibility of voluntary donations *mortis causa*: land was to pass to the legally determined person (this principle became especially strict from the reign of Henry II). This same lack of interest in the deceased's will on the part of the ordinary courts gradually led them to refrain from intervening in the distribution of personal property, so that the testator remained free to determine its future owner. It made possible the growth of ecclesiastical jurisdiction within the area left open. Unable to affect the destiny of real estate, the Church concentrated its efforts on controlling the future of personal property, with the aim of ensuring that at least a part of such property would be dedicated to pious purposes.

---

legacies and their proof through witnesses, without need of a written document.

[16] See M.M. Sheehan, *The Will in Medieval England*, 135 et seq.

This course of events moved the Church to assert authority over intestacy, in order to keep the lord from taking the chattels of the deceased. Moreover, there was a second reason for the Church's interest in intestacy: the religious character attributed to the will. To die without a will was often the equivalent to dying without confession, i.e. to die in sin. Therefore, when a person died without declaring a last will, the spiritual power assumed supervising over the distribution of his belongings, in order to guard over the well being of his soul. Thus, after the required distributions to relatives, the ecclesiastical power took a portion of the remaining property (normally a third) for use in works it considered appropriate[17].

The Crown rapidly recognized the ecclesiastical jurisdiction over intestate inheritance. The first draft of the Magna Carta made specific reference to it, namely: "Si aliquis liber homo intestatus decessit, catalla sua per manum propinquorum et amicorum suorum per visum Ecclesiæ distribuantur, salvis cuicunque debitis, quæ defunctus ei debebat"[18]. Even though this clause was absent in later versions, the Church's competence does not appear to have been questioned afterwards[19].

In any event, dying intestate was often considered a matter of dishonor in those times, whenever it was a consequence of the dying person's refusal to receive the sacraments and to give the appropriate directions regarding the payment of his debts and the future support of his wife and children. The Church urged the dying to leave an express will and to donate part of their wealth for pious causes. Not rarely that declaration of one's last will was the epilogue to the last confession,

---

[17] See C. Gross, "The Medieval Law of Intestacy", in *Select essays in Anglo-American legal history*, vol. 3, 723 et seq.

[18] "If a free man dies intestate, his chattels must be distributed by the hands of his relatives and friends, under the supervision of the Church, once his debts have been paid". Clause 27 of Magna Carta, cited by T.E. Scrutton, *The Influence of the Roman Law*, 167.

[19] This is the opinion of Maitland, who cites, as support, a passage by Bracton (see F. Pollock / F.W. Maitland, *History of English Law*, vol. 2, 356 et seq.).

and it was relatively informal, made in the presence of a priest and a few other witnesses. Because of this, and also as a result of the common law courts' lack of interference, testamentary issues gradually came under the umbrella of ecclesiastical jurisdiction.

In practice, the entire jurisdiction over the will fell into the hands of the Church authorities, who developed a complete procedure in this area: proof of the testator's will, inventory of possessions, review of accounts, etc. Thus canonical doctrine regarding testaments progressively gained a firm place in the life of medieval England[20].

That canonical doctrine was certainly based on Roman law, but it also possessed a number of distinctive features which contrasted with the older approach to succession, above all in issues related to the required formalities. With the intent of facilitating the effectiveness of last wills made *in articulo mortis*, canon law accepted the validity of oral wills declared in the presence of two witnesses. The written document was not an indispensable requisite — it was rather considered "another witness". The English ecclesiastical courts even came to permit verbal revocation of a written testament[21]. Moreover, they had a tendency to widen the circle of persons who were permitted to act as witnesses — for example, they admitted the testimony of women, contrary to a text in Gratian's *Decretum*[22].

Along with all the aforementioned, the Church courts extended their probate jurisdiction, i.e. matters relating to the proof of validity and

---

[20] The ecclesiastical testamentary jurisdiction became so deeply rooted in England, that the canonical doctrine had a remarkable influence in those local courts which, for a certain period of time, retained some jurisdiction over wills (see M.M. Sheehan, *Canon Law and English Institutions*, 392 et seq., and *The Will in Medieval England*, 207 et seq.).

[21] That practice would be transplanted to the common law courts when they began to enforce wills of land after 1540, though the practice would be interrupted by the Statute of Frauds enacted in 1677 (see R.H. Helmholz, *The English Law of Wills*, 207 et seq.).

[22] J.L. Barton, *Roman Law in England*, 87 et seq.; M.M. Sheehan, *The Will in Medieval England*, 176 et seq.

content of the testament. Initially, probate emerged as a procedure used only in cases of conflict — when litigation arose regarding the validity of the testament itself or the content of its dispositions. From the end of the twelfth century, however, probate ceased to be used strictly in adversarial proceedings and became a standard procedure prior to the administration of last wills[23]. The efficacy of English ecclesiastical courts on this matter is suggested by the fact that they retained this jurisdiction until the nineteenth century[24].

2. Extension and Limits of Ecclesiastical Jurisdiction

As a result of their jurisdictional activity in this field, ecclesiastical courts developed two institutions which would become central features of English succession law: the executor and the administrator[25].

The executor is remotely related to the Germanic *salmann*. However, his implantation as the main figure in testamentary execution in England occurred, without doubt, as a result of the action of the Church courts[26].

---

[23] M.M. Sheehan, *The Will in Medieval England*, 196 et seq.

[24] As mentioned before, the Court of Probate was created in 1857, inheriting the jurisdiction of the ecclesiastical courts on the matter.

[25] As Buckland has written, "our executor and administrator resemble the Roman *heres* much more than does our heir" (W.W. Buckland / A.D. Mc Nair, *Roman Law and Common Law*, 148).

[26] See on this subject, in addition to the general works on the history of English law, J.L. Barton, *Roman Law in England*, 82 et seq.; O.W. Holmes, "Executors in Earlier English Law", in *Select Essays in Anglo-American Legal History*", vol. 3, 737 et seq.; W.R. Jones, *Relations of the Two Jurisdictions*, 169 et seq.; M.M. Sheehan, *The Will in Medieval England*, 148 et seq.

The figure of the executor extended throughout Europe, due to the action of the ecclesiastical jurisdiction, in a relatively uniform manner and approximately in the same period of time. See R. Caillemer, *Origines et développement de l'exécution testamentaire* (Lyon, 1901); excerpts from that

Administration of a testament entailed carrying out a series of tasks. The obvious first step was authentication of the testator's will and determination of the intended recipients of his personal property. However, often it was also necessary to assemble and preserve that property in order for the various legacies to be paid. This, in turn, required settling the accounts of the personal estate — especially, preparing an inventory, collecting accounts receivable and paying off accounts payable. Only then was it possible to proceed to implementation of the will itself.

These activities required an individual to take charge of the testator's affairs posthumously. This individual was the executor, and his appointment was confirmed by the ecclesiastical authority, under whose jurisdiction the process was handled. In a way, it can even be affirmed that ecclesiastical jurisdiction over the implementation of wills developed and survived to the extent that the Church was able to strengthen and control the functions of the executor.

During the twelfth and thirteenth centuries the Church's role remained unquestioned. The ecclesiastical courts presided over lawsuits pertaining to the testator's existing debts or repayment of outstanding loans, with the acquiescence — whether by inaction or indifference — of the common law courts. In these lawsuits the executor was the person with standing to sue and be sued. In other words, under the auspices of ecclesiastical jurisdiction, the executor became the full representative of the testator, and with such a degree of success that the figure of the heir was relegated to a secondary plane.

Ecclesiastical monopoly, however, began to crumble from approximately the end of the thirteenth century. The second statute of Westminster (1285) marked the beginning of a process by which the common law absorbed the figure of the executor. This process was continued by a number of legislative dispositions which, through the concession of new writs, succeeded in permitting lawsuits by or against

---

work, with special reference to the English legal history, were published under the title of "The Executor in England and on the Continent", in *Select Essays in Anglo-American Legal History*, vol. 3, 746 et seq.

the executor to be brought before common law courts. That change of jurisdiction was aided by the pressure of the royal courts themselves, which displayed a growing interest in attracting the testamentary field to their own jurisdiction.

Half way through the fourteenth century, during the reign of Edward III, the institution of the executor had become part of the common law[27]. And there the institution remained — although for a certain period the common law had to share it with the ecclesiastical courts — keeping many of the characteristics and operative faculties that it had previously taken over from the Church courts[28]. The figure of the executor, in his capacity as representative of the testator, is one of the clearest canonical creations, which was subsequently transplanted to English law of succession, where it has survived with its original features largely intact, just as in North American law[29].

The introduction of the figure of the administrator occurred along similar channels[30]. The position was created in parallel fashion to that of the executor in the context of the canon law of intestacy, and was the

---

[27] See W.R. Jones, *Relations of the Two Jurisdictions*, 174 et seq.

[28] Actually the jurisdiction over testamentary debts was shared by the common law with the ecclesiastical courts throughout the rest of the Middle Ages, and perhaps even into the seventeenth century. However, at the moment it is not possible to fix precisely the pace at which testamentary jurisdiction was taken over by the secular courts. This is something which can only be revealed by a detailed historical investigation of the records of ecclesiastical and common law courts. For similar reasons, we do not know yet how extensively the common law courts assimilated the legal doctrine and practice previously elaborated by the ecclesiastical courts.

[29] Succession law on the European continent experienced an evolution in the opposite direction: from the sixteenth century on, there was a progressive return to the romanistic idea that the properties of the deceased — in case of intestacy as well as when there was an express will — were to be transferred to the heirs and administered by them, under judicial supervision (see H.J. Berman, *Law and Revolution*, 234).

[30] See W.R. Jones, *Relations of the Two Jurisdictions*, 176 et seq.

result of the practical of distributing the deceased's property where the person had died without leaving a last will.

It has already been noted that the ecclesiastical courts gained jurisdiction over intestacy in England very early. In these situations, it became necessary to establish a procedure of execution similar to the one performed in the case of wills. There was a need to appoint someone to step into the shoes of the deceased for purposes of administering his property. This person was called the administrator and was appointed and supervised by delegation of the bishop. His activities — as in the case of the executor — were conducted under the control of ecclesiastical jurisdiction during the first centuries of the common law system.

However, once again, the royal courts would eventually absorb the jurisdiction initially exercised by the Church. The beginning of this process was again marked by the second Statute of Westminster (1285), which made the bishop responsible for the debts of the deceased before the common law courts, either personally or through persons he designated as administrators. By 1357, the figure of the administrator had already been placed under the control of the common law. In that year, the bishop was required by statute to delegate his duties to one or more administrators, who were considered absolute representatives of the deceased and who were therefore granted the same rights and duties that the latter would have had[31].

From the prior statements one might infer that from the second half of the fourteenth century the common law took over a substantial part of the ecclesiastical jurisdiction in matters of succession. Reality, however, was not so simple. First, we must not forget that the Church of England preserved its jurisdiction over probate until 1857. Moreover, for a long period of time, ecclesiastical courts actually continued to exercise jurisdiction over a significant portion of testamentary debts, despite their theoretical transfer to the domain of the common law.

This fact was particularly clear in the case of debts which originated from contracts that did not fulfil the formalities required by the common

---

[31] F. Pollock / F.W. Maitland, *History of English Law*, vol. 2, 361.

law, especially verbal contracts, which could not be proved by deed. In these cases, royal courts afforded inadequate protection prior to the birth of the action of *assumpsit*[32] at the turn of the fifteenth to the sixteenth centuries. The party injured by breach of contract could only obtain a remedy through the ecclesiastical courts or the Court of Chancery, since these two institutions were significantly more flexible in the mechanisms accepted for proving contracts (and this flexibility was presumably a consequence of the influence of the canon law doctrine regarding *pacta nuda*). The involvement of ecclesiastical courts remained necessary to fill the gaps left by the common law of testamentary succession.

The Church's commitment did not end there, however. Other kinds of testamentary debts continued to be enforced in the ecclesiastical courts after the fourteenth century. People had come to rely on the effectiveness of their jurisdiction in these conflicts, and old habits died hard. The mere adoption of a legislative norm was not sufficient to change these established social habits. Quite to the contrary, a review of ecclesiastical archives of the time confirms that, despite the writs of prohibition emanating from common law courts, ecclesiastical courts continued to intervene in testamentary debts for a long period of time. Their intervention would only begin to decline sharply during the early sixteenth century, within the context of a profound change of social attitude towards the function of spiritual power[33].

[32] In chapter 8, I shall refer in detail to the action of *assumpsit*, which played a central role in the evolution of the English law of contract.

[33] The reach of the ecclesiastical jurisdiction over testamentary debts, and the reasons why it was preserved for such a long time, has been well described by R.H. Helmholz, "Debt Claims and Probate Jurisdiction in Historical Perspective", in *Canon Law and the Law of England*, 307 et seq. The author here remarks — as he has done in other writings — that it is absolutely necessary to resort to the ecclesiastical archives to obtain a realistic view of the English juridical scenario during the Middle Ages — the exclusive use of secular jurisdiction sources would provide an incomplete, and therefore distorted, image.

Up to now we have seen some important elements that ecclesiastical jurisdiction introduced into the English law of succession growing from the premise that the wishes of the testator were to be respected as sacred. In this regard, we could add two further details which, though not as significant, have remained in Anglo-American law to this day. First is the fact that when a corporation that does not have the legal capacity to own property is designated as legatee, the judge appoints a trustee to administer the legacy in its name. Second is the so-called *cy pres* doctrine (from the old Norman French, "as near as"): when the terms of a will, through impossibility or illegitimacy, cannot be fulfilled, the court must take measures to achieve the testator's will as close as possible — for example, if the legatee is deceased, another person similar to the one chosen by the testator will take instead[34].

In other areas, however, ecclesiastical jurisdiction would lose the battle with the common law in trying to shape the law of wills according to canon law guidelines. This can be seen with particular clarity in two specific subjects: the restrictions imposed on certain individuals' capacity to make a will, and the testator's freedom to determine the future of his property.

In regard to the former, I have already noted that the Church's intervention in succession issues was motivated by its interest in obtaining legacies in alms, for pious causes. From that starting point it was useful to expand, as much as possible, the number of individuals who were free to dispose of their property. But the common law posed two obstacles on the road: when a married woman left a testament without the express consent of her husband, it was considered illegal; and a similar restriction was imposed on people of servile condition, unless they had received a privilege to do so (the villein or serf was not considered a "free man")[35].

---

[34] See H.J. Berman, *Law and Revolution*, 236

[35] M.M. Sheehan, *The Will in Medieval England*, 234 et seq.; see also, by the same author, *Canon Law and English Institutions*, 393 et seq., and *The Influence of Canon Law on the Property Rights of Married Women*, 118 et seq.

In both cases, and repeatedly during the Middle Ages, the Church exerted pressure on the royal courts to force them to grant the freedom of testation to these individuals. The resistance of common lawyers turned those efforts into a constant failure, at least if we look at the situation from the standpoint of positive law. Social reality, however, demonstrates that these persons — women, above all — were sometimes able to make gifts *mortis causa*, and that their wills were carried out in fact[36].

The second area where the Church had to bow to the common law rules is the liberty of the testator in selecting the recipient of his property. It is known that the canonists of the classical era, following the law of Justinian, defended the obligatory character of the *legitima pars* — i.e. the percentage of the property of the deceased that had to be preserved for the widow and the children. For a time, the "legitim" was in force in England, though presumably rather as a result of local custom than by virtue of its protection by the ecclesiastical jurisdiction. However, towards the end of the fourteenth century, the use of the *legitima* decreased rapidly in favor of the unrestricted freedom of will. There are two probable causes of this decay: either the ecclesiastical courts lacked adequate means of imposing official canonical doctrine, or they did not have enough interest in doing so. The truth of the matter is that the common law continued to ignore the right of the deceased's relatives to a part of his inheritance[37].

---

[36] M.M. Sheehan, *The Influence of Canon Law on the Property Rights of Married Women*, 118 et seq. Sheehan notes that, in the fourteenth century, some local courts endorsed the testament of villeins.

[37] See R.H. Helmholz, "*Legitim* in English Legal History", in *Canon law and the law of England*, 247 et seq.; M.M. Sheehan, *The Influence of Canon Law on the Property Rights of Married Women*, 117 et seq. Sheehan maintains that the Church, until the fourteenth century, invested a considerable effort to have the common law accepting the *legitima*, especially as far as the rights of the widows were concerned. From the fourteenth century on, Helmholz tends to consider that the disappearance of the "legitim" was a deviation of English ecclesiastical practice from the canon law of pontifical sources.

Testamentary freedom, though appreciably cut back by the Inheritance (Family Provision) Act in 1938, survived in English law for a long time, contrary to what is habitual in continental legal systems. On the other hand, the legal restrictions on the capacity of some men and women to leave a will would eventually disappear as the principle of equality before the law became more fully realized. Here again, medieval canon law anticipated solutions which the common law would adopt much later.

Chapter 8

Contract Law

The possible influence of canon law on the development of contract theory in the common law is a subject that has been extensively studied by Anglo-American legal historians[1]. The discussion has centered mostly around two institutions which occupy a pivotal place in the evolution of English contract law: the action of *assumpsit*, which became the principal element of unification of the law of contract from

[1] Although there have been valuable contributions by other authors from the last century, the most significant study of this subject has been accomplished by: W.T. Barbour, "The History of Contract in Early English Equity", in P. Vinogradoff, ed, *Oxford Studies in Social and Legal History*, vol. 4, (New York, 1974; reprint of the 1st ed, 1914); J. Gordley, *The Philosophical Origins of Modern Contract Doctrine* (Oxford, 1991), and "Natural Law Origins of the Common Law of Contract", in J. Barton, ed, *Towards a General Law of Contract* (Berlin, 1990), 367 et seq.; R.H. Helmholz, "Assumpsit and *fidei læsio*", in *Canon Law and the Law of England*, 263 et seq., and "Contracts and the Canon Law: Possible Points of Contact between England and the Continent", in J. Barton, ed, *Towards a General Law of Contract*, 49 et seq.; and A.W.B. Simpson, *A History of the Common Law of Contract. The Rise of the Action of Assumpsit* (Oxford, 1975), and "The Equitable Doctrine of Consideration and the Law of Uses", *16 University of Toronto Law Journal*1 et seq. (1965).

the early seventeenth century; and the doctrine of consideration, which has been described as "the essence of the common law of contract"[2].

1. Assumpsit, Consideration and Canon Law

During the first centuries of its development, the common law provided a limited protection for contracts. Adequate protection was only available when the contract could be proved by a written instrument[3]. If one did not exist or had been lost, the party injured by a breach of contract had to resort to other jurisdictions for a remedy, namely the Court of Chancery, the local courts or the ecclesiastical courts. The latter, however, had been forbidden from interfering in contractual matters on the basis of breach of faith when the underlying transaction qualified as "debt" (i.e. when the obligation consisted in paying a sum of money, or providing a determined quantity of fungibles). In addition, the system of local justice was undergoing an incessant decline in favor of royal courts.

From the fifteenth century onwards, the common law courts began to increase the level of protection granted to informal contracts through the action of *assumpsit*. This term indicated acceptance of a peculiar

---

[2] S.F.C. Milsom, *Historical Foundations*, 356.

[3] At the beginnings of the common law other means of proof were admitted: principally, wager of law or compurgation, a procedure taken from the practice of local courts. In it the defendant denied, under oath, that he had any obligation whatsoever with regard to the plaintiff, and brought forward another eleven persons (compurgators) who would swear the same in his support. That procedure was widespread in medieval England, and was also used by ecclesiastical courts, especially in criminal cases: see R.H. Helmholz, "Crime, Compurgation and the Courts of the Medieval Church", in *Canon law and the law of England*, 119 et seq., and more recently, by the same author, *The Spirit of Classical Canon Law* (The University of Georgia Press, 1996), 158-159. Nevertheless, compurgation proved much less efficient in the royal courts of Westminster than in local courts: in London it was not difficult for the defendant to find compurgators willing to swear falsely for a sum of money.

commitment, whereby one of the contracting parties by his promise expressly assumed the responsibility for non performance. Initially, however, *assumpsit* had only a limited application, as a variant of the "action on the case". It was not even conceived as a contractual action, but rather, within the domain of torts, as an action meant to obtain compensatory damages. Notwithstanding its lowly births, *assumpsit* experienced an uninterrupted process of growth, eventually becoming the habitual action for all kinds of breaches of contract — including parol contracts — especially from *Slade's case*, in 1602[4].

On the other hand, from the mid-sixteenth century, the action of *assumpsit* for breach of promise came to be associated with the doctrine of consideration — i.e. the sum of the elements inducing a person to enter into a given contract or agreement. The presence — or absence — of consideration became a threshold test to determine whether an action of *assumpsit* would lie. It meant that not all promises were actionable. Only those promises where there was sufficient "consideration" gave rise to *assumpsit*[5].

---

[4] In addition to the works of Barbour and Simpson cited in note 75, an accurate exposition of this phase of English contractual law can be found in the classic treatises of Holdsworth, Plucknett and Pollock/Maitland; and also in three of the works published in the third volume of the *Select Essays in Anglo-American Legal History*, repeatedly cited in this book: J.B. Ames, "The History of Parol Contracts prior to *Assumpsit*", 304 et seq., and "The History of *Assumpsit*", 259 et seq.; and J.W. Salmond, *The History of Contract*, 320 et seq. For a more updated study, see: J.H. Baker, *An introduction to English Legal History*, 263 et seq.; S.F.C. Milsom, *Historical Foundations*, 314 et seq.; W.M. McGovern, "Contract in Medieval England: The Necessity for *Quid Pro Quo* and a Sum Certain", 13 *The American Journal of Legal History*, 173 et seq. (1969).

[5] It is thus explained by Simpson: "The consideration, or considerations, for a promise meant the factors which the promisor considered when he promised, and which moved or motivated his promising. Although not a precise equivalent, "motive" is perhaps as near as one can get by way of synonym. The essence of the doctrine of consideration, then, is the adoption by the common law of the idea that the legal effect of a promise should depend upon the factor or factors which motivated the promise. To decide

It is not difficult to see a parallelism between canon law and these institutions of English contractual law. The views adopted by canonists on contract theory during the Later Middle Ages can be summarized as follows[6].The obligation to perform a contract — and consequently its enforceability — depended on the existence of a mutual commitment between the parties deriving from a licit cause, rather than merely on compliance with any formal requisite. Hence the *pacta nuda* ("naked contracts") should be afforded judicial protection if the *causa* for them could be proved. Furthermore, when the mutual promise was accompanied by an oath, as often happened, a remedy could be sought before ecclesiastical courts on the basis of a breach of the faith pledged in the oath, or *fidei læsio*, considered as a moral offence[7].

Thus, the development of the action of *assumpsit* is very similar to the canonical insistence on protecting the *pacta nuda* in those cases where an oath was breached, in contrast to the Roman law principle *ex nudo pacto non oritur actio* ("from a nude pact no action can arise"), that had been taken over by Bracton[8]. Likewise, the doctrine of consideration appears analogous to the notion of *causa*, which medieval canonists adapted from the Roman law of Justinian. Like consideration, the *causa* served as a floodgate to limit those cases in which the *pacta nuda* would be actionable — actionability was extended only to those *pacta* which were seriously intended[9].

---

whether a promise to do X is binding, you need to know why the promise was made" (A.W.B. Simpson, *A History of the Common Law of Contract*, 321).

[6] See R. Zimmermann, *The Law of Obligations. Roman Foundations of the Civilian Tradition* (Cape Town & Munchen, 1992), 542 et seq.

[7] See R.H. Helmholz, *Contracts and the Canon Law*, 50 et seq., and the bibliography there cited.

[8] See F. Pollock / F.W. Maitland, *History of English Law*, vol. 2, 194 et seq.

[9] See. R. Zimmermann, *The Law of Obligations*, 549, who points out the probable influence of the scholastic doctrine of causation (especially St. Thomas Aquinas) on the doctrine of the classical canonists. Moreover, it seems to be a canonical re-elaboration of the Roman principle *pacta sunt*

It is well-known that these two concepts of canon law played an important role in the development of contractual theory on the Continent[10]. Some scholars have tried to prove that there was a similar canonical influence on the development of the common law of contract. According to this interpretation, the action of *assumpsit* and the doctrine of consideration were essentially the result of the influence of canon law on that area of English law[11], channeled through two institutions: the Court of Chancery and the ecclesiastical courts.

Barbour is perhaps the leading scholar who sought to explore the degree of canonical influence on the Court of Chancery, with documentary support coming from a careful work in the Chancery records[12]. He starts with a historical fact that is difficult to question: during the fifteenth century, Chancery protected parties injured as a

---

servanda, which would have a great significance in international public law, as another canonical contribution on this matter did: the *rebus sic stantibus* clause (which, however, tended to disappear from the law of contract in the nineteenth century: see ibid., 576 et seq.).

[10] See G. Le Bras, "Canon Law", in C.G. Crump / E.F. Jacobs Eds, *The Legacy of the Middle Ages* (Oxford, 1969; reprint of the 1st ed, 1926), 352 et seq.; J. Maldonado, *La significación histórica del Derecho canónico* (Madrid, 1969); R. Zimmermann, *The Law of Obligations*, 549 et seq. Zimmermann remarks that the importance of the notion of the cause in contract law declined from the seventeenth and eighteenth centuries, because among other reasons "by the time of the usus modernus pandectarum, causa had played out its historically most important role: namely that of facilitating the transition from a closed shop of (enforceable) pacta vestita to the principle of modern law that every agreement begets an action" (Ibid., 553).

[11] Among the classic authors, the canonical influence has been categorically rejected by Ames (see his works mentioned in note 78) and also by Holmes, who affirms that consideration is a simple modification of the ancient requisite of the *quid pro quo* in the action of debt. (O.W. Holmes, *Early English Equity*,17 et seq.).

[12] See W.T. Barbour, *The History of Contract in Early English Equity*, cited in note 75.

result of breaches of oral contracts, whereas no remedy was available to them through the common law[13].

Moreover, Chancellors determined the outcome of the cases on grounds of conscience, which often meant rendering obligations legally binding based on their ethical nature. Indeed, St. German's writings are a testimony to the degree of canonical influence on the Chancellor's use of conscience. In view of the numerous references by plaintiffs to a pledge of faith as the basis for their petition, it can be presumed that the Chancellor granted a remedy based upon breach of promise. At the same time, Barbour also observed that plaintiffs sometimes alluded to the existence of a "cause" sufficient to support what he claimed[14], and this fact seems to point to the canonical doctrine of *causa* as a criterion for selecting the promises which deserved judicial protection.

Based on this data, Barbour maintained the thesis that Chancery developed a comprehensive contract theory in regard to parole contracts, which — as most evidence suggests — was taken primarily from the canon law. The plausibility of Barbour's thesis is reinforced by the fact that the Chancellors of the time were churchmen and often also canonists. They were presumably familiar with the canonical doctrine regarding the role of *causa* and also conversant with the practices adopted by the Church courts in *fidei læsio* cases[15] (although Chancery and the ecclesiastical courts did not always act in identical fashion[16]).

---

[13] W.M. Mcgovern, "The Enforcement of Informal Contracts in the Later Middle Ages", 59 *California Law Review* 1144 et seq. (1971).

[14] It especially occurred in relation to contracts based on marriage: marriage itself was considered a "sufficient cause".

[15] It is significant that Holmes, despite rejecting that there was any canonical influence on the doctrine of consideration, admits that English Chancellors applied the same principles that guided ecclesiastical jurisdiction in *fidei læsio* causes (see O.W. Holmes, *Early English Equity*,23 et seq.).

[16] In this regard, it is interesting to note some differences between the practice of Chancery and that of the ecclesiastical courts. In Chancery — contrary to what occurred in *fidei læsio* cases —, although the specific performance of the contract was the remedy normally granted, sometimes the

If we now direct our attention to what was occurring in the common law, we observe that, during the sixteenth century, the action of *assumpsit* began to gain preeminence, probably in order to recover the jurisdiction over contractual disputes that had been assumed by Chancery. Taking into account the evident analogies between *assumpsit* and *fidei læsio*, as well as the parallel between consideration and *causa*, it is sensible to infer that common lawyers assumed not only the jurisdiction, but also the contractual theory developed and applied by the Chancellors. This affirmation — Barbour concluded — cannot be demonstrated with mathematical precision, but the evidence suggests an indirect reception of canon law through the Court of Chancery[17].

This thesis is undoubtedly attractive. However, Barbour himself acknowledged that there is an insurmountable difficulty in proving it in definitive fashion: the lack of sufficient documentation regarding Chancery's activities before the sixteenth century. This fact, in turn, creates a double obstacle: it generates uncertainty in relation to the exact reach of the equitable jurisdiction over contracts; and it hides the precise reasons behind the Chancellor's decisions[18]. In spite of this problem, Barbour's analysis has been accepted in one way or another

---

plaintiff was afforded compensatory damages. Moreover, the plaintiff did not always allege breach of promise, or the fact that the promise had been supported by an oath; on occasions the claim was based solely on "equity and good conscience". Evidence suggests that the Chancellor's jurisdiction on contracts was less linked to the strict principles of canon law than that of the ecclesiastical courts. To put it another way, Chancery utilized certain canonical principles, but was not limited by them — rather it granted remedy in equity with a larger capacity of operation (see R.H. Helmholz, *Contracts and the Canon Law*, 61).

[17] See W.T. Barbour, *The History of Contract in Early English Equity*, 168 et seq. Barbour provides an additional argument in support of his thesis: the fact that the Chancellors, obviously, did not follow the common law theory on contracts; in those circumstances, it is most probable that their source of inspiration was canon law.

[18] See ibid., 150 et seq. We should recall that the systematic record of the Chancery's decisions does not begin until Henry VIII's reign.

by most historians, although some of them have admitted a certain degree of reserve about fully embracing his conclusions[19].

More recently, Simpson has revisited the matter, giving special emphasis to possible connections between the doctrine of consideration and canon law[20]. He remarks that the unavoidable lack of documentary evidence makes it impossible to take Barbour's idea beyond the hypothetical plane. It is not possible to establish without doubt the origin of contractual doctrines used by medieval Chancellors, and consequently neither it is possible to defend the thesis that the doctrine of consideration has indisputable canonical origins[21].

In an attempt to identify the true source of inspiration for the development of the doctrine of consideration in English contractual law, Simpson claims to have found it in the so-called "equitable doctrine of consideration" applied in the law of uses, which, contrary to what its epithet might suggest, was developed by the common lawyers from the fifteenth century in connection with real property. That doctrine had been created to determine which factors made a consideration "good enough" to allow a use to be enforced. According to Simpson, it would have been adapted to contract law as a logical consequence of the necessity of deciding which promises would be enforceable in the action of *assumpsit*.

---

[19] But some others have accepted his conclusions as accurate. Holdsworth, for example, while underlining the peculiar slant given by the common lawyers to the doctrine of consideration, appears to share Barbour's views: "it may be said that the ideas drawn from the canon law and the practice of the ecclesiastical Chancellors were the greatest of the forces which inspired the common lawyers to create the most distinctive of all the features of the English law of contract — the doctrine of consideration" (W.S. Holdsworth, "The Early History of Equity", 13 *Michigan Law Review* 301 (1915).

[20] See A.W.B. Simpson, *A History of the Common Law of Contract*, cited in note 75.

[21] And — adds Simpson — the uncertainty grows stronger when one considers that apparently there was not a definite canonical doctrine on contractual *causa*, but rather an ensemble of differing opinions on the matter (see ibid., 376).

From that standpoint, Simpson examines another way in which canon law might have contributed to begetting and moulding the concept of consideration: the hypothesis that canonical influence would have come about indirectly through *Doctor and Student*. His analysis of St. German's work leads him to accept that, notwithstanding certain significant differences, there are noteworthy analogies with the contractual ideas contained in the *Summæ* of the medieval moralists. Nevertheless, in the end he reaches the conclusion that this hypothesis must be rejected, in light of the preexisting doctrine of consideration with regard to uses — it is more likely that common lawyers drew their ideas from within their own legal environment.

However, what is in fact likely — Simpson admits — is that the powerful impact of *Doctor and Student* helped to foster the extension of the doctrine of consideration into the framework of contractual law. Even so, he concludes that the doctrine of consideration finds its principal origins not in canon law, but rather in the common law itself[22].

Helmholz has shed some light on this question, from the different perspective provided by the study of ecclesiastical records[23]. Specifically, the North American historian tries to establish a causal link between the action of *assumpsit* and the *fidei læsio* causes which were heard by the English ecclesiastical courts. These causes — it has already been noted — were lawsuits directed at obtaining specific performance of a promise backed by an oath. Because perjury was a moral offence, the Church claimed there existed a sufficient basis to intervene in those cases, often resorting to the threat of excommunication as a means of enforcing fulfilment of the obligation.

In relation to the historical period which concerns us here, it is a fact that, despite the prohibition contained in the Constitutions of Clarendon, ecclesiastical courts continued to decide those causes during

---

[22] This opinion is shared by J.H. Baker, "Origins of the 'Doctrine' of Consideration", in *On the Laws and Customs of England. Essays in Honor of Samuel E. Thorne* (Chapel Hill, 1981), 351 et seq.

[23] See R.H. Helmholz, *Assumpsit and "Fidei Læsio"*, and *Contracts and the Canon Law*, both cited in note 75.

the fifteenth and part of the sixteenth century, and they did so according to the norms of canon law[24]. It is important to remark that those were precisely the years when *assumpsit* was coming into being as a truly contractual action. Moreover, the comparison of this action with the *causæ fidei læsionis* reveals significant analogies, both from the standpoint of procedure and substance. In *assumpsit* and *fidei læsio* causes, the sort of promises enforced consisted of relatively informal, oral agreements; and the comparative examination of secular and ecclesiastical records discloses significant coincidences — even in terminology — as far as the pleadings are concerned [25].

The chronology of events also offers suggestive piece of information — there was a direct correlation between the rise of the action of *assumpsit* in the common law courts and the decrease of *fidei læsio* causes in the ecclesiastical courts. The competence of the latter in this matter seems to have disappeared by the mid-sixteenth century. Although it is not possible to go beyond a conjectural level, Helmholz is inclined to accept what is suggested by this coincidence: the development of *assumpsit* — without underrating Barbour's thesis — appears to have been caused by the decline of the *fidei læsio*[26], not by

[24] This occurred as much in England as on the Continent. Ecclesiastical courts tended to put a particular emphasis on the canonical doctrine of the cause (*causa*) of contracts, and habitually followed the summary procedure established by the decretal *Sæpe contingit* of Pope Clement V in 1306. The result of this was that the ecclesiastical jurisdiction relatively invaded the domain of the secular jurisdiction. The temporal power attempted to correct that situation via the *declinatio fori* on the Continent, and by means of the writ of prohibition in England; the success of this reaction was varying until the sixteenth century, when jurisdiction over that sort of contractual causes definitely passed to the secular forum (see R.H. Helmholz, *Contracts and the Canon Law*, 57 et seq.)

[25] See ibid., 62 et seq.

[26] In this regard, it is significant that Baker, in spite of rejecting the canonical origin of the doctrine of consideration, has acknowledged that it is not possible to understand the success of the actions on the case by breach of promise if we ignore the decline of the *læsio fidei* (J.H. Baker, introduction to *The Reports of Sir John Spelman*, 257 et seq.).

way of a simple chain of events, but rather as an actual transfer of procedural remedies from the ecclesiastical to the secular forum. For the rest, this event is not at all strange in the context of the process of secularization experienced by England during the sixteenth century[27].

Personally, I do not think that the present state of historical investigation allows one to draw more precise conclusions. Whether the action of *assumpsit* and the doctrine of consideration were the result of canon law influence, or rather emerged from within the common law, will likely remain one more of those secrets which are zealously guarded by history. Indeed, it is probable that neither extreme may be entirely correct. As is the case with most legal institutions, native elements are amalgamated with others taken from a more elaborate body of law, with which they have come into contact[28]. Certainly, the sum of information provided by Barbour and Helmholz leads us to believe that these two central elements of contract law were not an absolutely original or independent creation of the common lawyers[29]. This conclusion is reinforced if we take into account that the common

---

[27] Helmholz, however, remarks that there was not a complete reception of the solutions adopted by the ecclesiastical courts. Some of the features which characterize the action of *assumpsit* in its definitive consolidation through the sixteenth century have their origin in the common law rather than in canon law — especially the fact that it was necessary to plead and prove that the damage suffered by the plaintiff was a consequence of the defective fulfilment of the contract by the defendant (and this is something which recalls the character of the action of *assumpsit* in its inception). See R.H. Helmholz, *Contracts and the Canon Law*, 63 et seq.

[28] In this regard, as far as consideration is concerned, see J.L. Barton, "The Early History of Consideration", 85 *Law Quarterly Review* 372 et seq. (1969).

[29] On the other hand, it is interesting to note that, Zimmermann, incidentally, points out that the idea of *causa* reappeared in Lord Mansfield's moral consideration theory: Lord Mansfield, the towering figure on the English legal scene in the second half of the eighteenth century, had attended lectures on Roman law at Oxford and was thus familiar with civil law ideas; his Scottish background may have contributed too (R. Zimmermann, *The Law of Obligations*, 506).

law has been influenced by Roman and canon law even in certain areas of the law of the obligations to which it had previously adopted a decidedly antagonistic attitude[30].

Whatever the case may be, the difficulty of offering a satisfactory reply to this question should not cause us to lose sight of other aspects of Anglo-American contract law where we can also observe the influence of canon law.

2. Other Elements of Roman-Canonical Origin

Simpson has noted that, in the fourteenth century, ecclesiastical doctrine on usury was followed in relation to penal money bonds incorporated into loan agreements. Penal bonds were a form of guarantee by which the borrower was obliged to pledge to pay a sum to the lender in excess of the borrowed amount if the loan was not repaid on maturity. Medieval canonists defended this obligation as licit, because it was destined to compensate the creditor for the *damnum emergens* (similar to consequential damages) and the *lucrum cessans* (lost profits) caused by the delay. Its usurious character was discounted by the fact that the monetary penalty arose only if repayment was not made at maturity. Despite medieval society's sensitivity toward usury, these concepts were accepted by the royal courts[31].

---

[30] It is again Zimmermann who offers an illustrative example, although, strictly speaking, alien to the law of contract. The Anglo-American tradition did not embrace the romanistic doctrine of the *negotiorum gestio* (he who takes charge of another's *negotium* not acting in his own interest, even without the mediation of a contract of mandate, can recover from the beneficiary for the damage that he has suffered). Nevertheless, it is generally accepted that a stranger who has buried a deceased may recover his reasonable expenses from the person primarily responsible for the burial. This rule appears to be based on the Roman *actio funeraria*, and it came to England via the jurisdiction of the medieval ecclesiastical courts (R. Zimmermann, *The Law of Obligations*, 448).

[31] See A.W.B. Simpson, *A History of the Common Law of Contract*, 113 et seq. Usury, moreover, was under the jurisdiction of ecclesiastical courts in

After all, these situations were treated according to one of the fundamental principles of classical canon law on contractual matters: the principle of *pretium iustum* (fair or "just" price). The idea defended by canonists and civilians alike was that, in all contracts, the things or services exchanged should possess comparable value. That did not prevent a person from obtaining benefits from a contract. What was condemned was the *turpe lucrum* (unfair or "shameful" profit), as this was identified with avaricious business practices. That was the reason why usury was prohibited. For the same reason, a number of different types of financing operations and credit devices, in which interest was charged for the lending of money, ceased to be considered usurious, as the economies of the West saw greater levels of mercantile activity, and loans were increasingly made for large-scale economic enterprises, and not simply for the subsistence of individuals or families, as had occurred in a society whose economy was based solely on agriculture. This change in the canonists' attitude presupposed the transformation of the Roman contract of deposit into a loan of money for investment, with an optional rate of interest; and, insofar as these practices became legitimized by canon law, a new and important base for the development of mercantile and financial activity in Europe came into being[32].

In another context, we can observe how the Court of Chancery received the influence of the canonical doctrine concerning the regulation of error — namely in determining the cases in which error constitutes a sufficient ground to invalidate legal acts — elaborated, to a great extent, in relation to matrimonial contracts. Within the common law system, error had no legal significance. In equity, while the *error iuris* (error in law) was also of no relevance, the rule was exactly the

---

England until the end of the Middle Ages (R.H. Helmholz, "Usury and Medieval English Courts", in *Canon law and the Law of England*, 323 et seq.).

[32] See. H.J. Berman, *Law and Revolution*, 247 et seq.; J.T. Gilchrist, *The Church and Economic Activity in the Middle Ages* (New York, 1969), 107 et seq. and 274 et seq.; J. Noonan, *The Scholastic Analysis of Usury* (Cambridge, Mass., 1957), especially 506 et seq.

opposite with regard to the *error facti* (error in fact). Chancery would even modify the written terms of an existing deed, with the goal of reflecting the real intent of the parties.

Spence has attributed that attitude of Chancery to a Roman law origin, more specifically to the *Digest*[33]. In my opinion, it is more likely that its direct source of inspiration was the 13th *regula iuris* of Pope Boniface VIII's *Liber Sextus*, according to which "ignorantia facti, non iuris, excusat" ("the ignorance of facts is a valid excuse, but not so the ignorance of the law")[34]. In any event, it does not appear to be merely coincidental that, from the beginning of the seventeenth century, the common law courts began to apply a similar doctrine in regard to the action of *indebitatus assumpsit* in cases where monetary payments had been made by mistake[35].

In addition, one of the most distinctive characteristics of Chancery's treatment of contracts, the doctrine of specific performance, seems to be of canonical origin. It is clear that the specific performance doctrine does not proceed from the common law, which followed the guidelines of Roman law in this matter: in the event of a breach, the judge only had power to grant compensatory damages, as stated in the aphorism "nemo potest præcise cogi ad factum". This led Spence to describe the doctrine of specific performance as a "clerical invention" of the English Chancellors, who would have departed on this point from the practice

---

[33] G. Spence, *Equitable Jurisdiction*, vol. 1, 631 et seq.

[34] This opinion is reinforced by the fact that Chancery did not always apply the Roman doctrine of the irrelevance of the *error facti* caused by negligence, expressed in the *Digest*'s maxim "nec stultis solere succurri, sed errantibus" (what may be translated as "mistaken people, but not foolish people, deserve to be helped"). Thus, when that Roman doctrine was alleged before Chancellor Stillington on a certain occasion, he replied with another maxim frequently used in the Chancery: "Deus est procurator fatuorum" ("God is fatuous peoples' attorney"). The case related to a mortgage that had been paid without demanding a written receipt; Stillington ordered the mortgage to be canceled (the case is cited by Spence, *Equitable Jurisdiction*, vol. 1, 636).

[35] See J.H. Baker, *An Introduction to English Legal History*, 307 et seq.

of the Roman prætors, their source of inspiration in many other respects[36]. Seeking to identify the canonical source more specifically, Fry has pointed to Gregory IX's decretals[37], where it is provided that "studiose agendum est, ut ea, quæ promittuntur, opere compleantur"[38]. In any event, we cannot ignore the parallelism of specific performance with the canonical principle which states that a penitent should not be absolved until he has fulfilled his promise, a principle which could hardly been unknown to ecclesiastical Chancellors, and which presumably influenced their conception of the duties of conscience being applied in the Court of Chancery[39].

Also, in the matter of suretyship (personal guarantees for the fulfilment of a contract), English law appears to have experienced the influence of Roman-canonical law through the Chancery jurisdiction. In particular, the rules relating to the Roman *fideiussio* seem to have shaped the accessory nature of the surety's liability; and the *beneficium cedendarum actionum* lives on the form of a duty of contribution between co-sureties and of the doctrine of subrogation[40].

On the whole, that English law should have incorporated Roman-canonical elements in relation to contract law is by no means strange. We should not forget that for the medieval common law — a clearly feudal concept of law — the objective relationship between individuals constituted the primary source of legal obligation. For this reason, as the common law began to regulate contracts in a more detailed manner, it is

---

[36] G. Spence, *Equitable Jurisdiction*, vol. 1, 645.

[37] See E. Fry, *A Treatise on the Specific Performance of Contracts* (London, 2d ed,1881), 3-8 (cited by T.E. Scrutton, *The Influence of the Roman Law*, 161).

[38] *Decretalium D. Gregorii Papæ IX*, lib. I, tit. XXXV (*De pactis*), chap. III (according to the edition of Friedberg / Richter, vol. 2, 204).

[39] See R. Zimmermann, *The Law of Obligations*, 776 et seq.

[40] See A Kiralfy, "History of the Law of Personal Guarantee (Suretyship) in England since 1500", 29*Recueils de la Société Jean Bodin pour l'Histoire Comparative des Institutions* 400 (1971); R. Zimmermann, *The Law of Obligations*, 144 et seq.

understandable that it should have directed its attention towards the Roman law as shaped by the legists and canonists of the Middle Ages: the contract was a specific relationship based on the voluntary commitment of the parties, and the idea of free will was precisely the axis around which the whole Roman legal system turned.

It is worth recalling, moreover, that the influence of canonical doctrines on Anglo-American contractual law extended beyond the Middle Ages, especially in the works of North American jurists. When the common lawyers of the nineteenth century became attracted to the rationalist school of natural law, they were also opening up entry to ideas which, to a large extent, had shaped that school — the theological and legal doctrines of the Spanish scholastics of the sixteenth and early seventeenth centuries, whose connections with the medieval University tradition is sufficiently well-known to require no comment here[41]. Gordley has recently stressed that influence, and indicated some aspects of modern Anglo-American contractual theory that originated from those sources: for example, the notion that the contract is essentially based on consent, or the rule stating that offers are not totally binding until they are accepted[42].

In one way or another, virtually every time that Anglo-American jurists have felt the necessity to systematize their ideas on contract law, they have turned towards legal constructs rooted in the Roman-canonical heritage. In this regard, it is significant that Blackstone, the first writer to attempt a comprehensive and coherent look at the common law on contracts, drew his inspiration from the work of an Italian professor of civil and canon law: Giovanni Vincenzo Gravina[43].

---

[41] See F. Wieacker, "The Importance of Roman Law for Western Civilization and Western Legal Thought", 4 *Boston College International and Comparative Law Review* 260 et seq. (1981).

[42] See J. Gordley, *Natural Law Origins of the Common Law of Contract*, 423 et seq., 447 et seq.; and *The Philosophical Origins of Modern Contract Doctrine*, 134 et seq.

[43] T.F.T Plucknett, *Concise History*, 652. Gordley, on the other hand, transmits an interesting observation in relation to the canonical notion of

Naturally, it would be incorrect to conclude that Anglo-American contract law — as any other specific area of the common law tradition — is no more than a by-product of the civil law tradition. It is undeniable that contract is one of the fields where the common law displays a definite personality of its own vis-à-vis continental law. But it would be inaccurate to presume that the reason for that originality was a radical insularity of the common law of contract, or that it came exclusively from inside the British Isles. In my opinion, what the common lawyers did was rather to absorb the ideas they needed at particular points in time, and to give those ideas a renewed vitality by incorporating them into their own legal system.

---

causa and the English concept of consideration. In his opininon, those concepts are totally different, in regard to their origin as well as to their function. Nevertheless, starting from Bracton, every time the common lawyers wanted to develop a systematic theory of consideration, they persisted in remarking the parallelism between the concepts of consideration and *causa* (see J. Gordley, *Natural Law Origins of the Common Law of Contract*, 437 et seq., and *The Philosophical Origins of Modern Contract Doctrine*, 138).

Chapter 9

Constitutional Law and Theory

At the very outset of our exploration into the influence of canon law on the development of English constitutional law we encounter an initial difficulty: it is problematic to mark out the boundaries of the constitutional domain in England, as Maitland stressed years ago, because of the absence of a Constitution in the formal sense of the term and a consequent lack of clear definition of the laws which qualify as constitutional[1]. Furthermore, a radically insular perspective has been traditional among Anglo-American historians in this field; generally, scholars have focused attention only on events in Great Britain, paying relatively little attention to their connections with what was occurring on the Continent[2]. If we add to these two limitations the especial

---

[1] F.W. Maitland, *The Constitutional History of England* (Cambridge, 1961; reprint of the 1st ed, 1908), 536 et seq. Maitland remarks that, because of it, the definition of constitutional law cannot be but a conventional one. In this regard, adopting a pragmatic point of view, the domain of constitutional law has been described as a group of mechanisms which not only serve to define the government, but also to limit its activity: see F.D. Wormuth, *The Origins of Modern Constitutionalism* (New York ,1949), 3.

[2] In this regard, and in addition to the already mentioned constitutional histories by Maitland, Stubbs and Wormuth, see, for example, the following two works of S.B. Chrimes, *English Constitutional History* (London, 3d ed,1965), and *English Constitutional Ideas* (New York, 1966); and these books of B.

characteristics of constitutional law vis-à-vis other areas of law it becomes difficult to assess with accuracy the effect of Roman and canonical ideas on the development of English constitutional law.

The task we undertake here might also be regarded perhaps as less relevant than in private law, since this is the area of English law which has failed to secure universal influence; its application has remained confined to the British Isles, and has had only a marginal influence on the common law tradition elsewhere.

In any event, and in spite of the undeniable limitations of English constitutional law, English legal evolution was not immune from the influence of theories and ideas developed by continental canonists and civilians. However, we must recognize that the existing deficiencies in historical investigation make it impossible to explore fully a topic as complex and broad as this one; therefore, the following discussion must necessarily be succinct.

Finally, I must highlight the fact that constitutional law is perhaps the area of law where legal rules, custom and the contributions of legal doctrine become most completely intermingled. It is not always easy to determine the degree to which a norm originates from the simple exercise of political power, from customary roots, or from the theories developed by legal scholars. The point is particularly relevant, since we are dealing with one of the fields in which legal doctrine — jurisprudence — has been most influential. To disregard it would be naive at best, and would surely produce a distorted image of reality.

Wilkinson, *Studies in the Constitutional History of the Thirteenth and Fourteenth Centuries* (Manchester, 2d ed,1952), *Constitutional History of England in the Fifteenth Century, 1399-1485* (New York, 1964). More recently there seems to be a change of attitude in some scholars towards a less insular perspective; see, for instance, J.G.A. Pocock, *The Ancient Constitution and the Feudal Law: A Study of English Constitutional Thought in the Seventeenth Century* (Cambridge, 2d ed, 1987).

1. Canonical Influence on the Great Constitutional Principles

We ought to commence with a well-known fact. The modern notion of State, as well as modern constitutional theory, does not arise *ex nihilo*, nor does it originate exclusively in the new ideas regarding man, power, and society which shook European life and thought during the fifteenth and sixteenth centuries. Quite the contrary, its origin can be traced back to the political theory and practice of the Middle Ages.

More specifically, the first practical realization of a modern State can be found — even if only in germinal form — in the new concept of the Church which was shaped by the Reform promoted by Pope Gregory VII in the last third of the eleventh century. The Church that emerged from the Gregorian Reform became, in effect, the first truly translocal authority in the West since the fall of the Roman Empire. The Church introduced the notion of a State ruled by law — government *through* law, and government *under* the law. In other words, the Church instituted a system in which the government used the law as its primary instrument of policy and control, and in which the ruler — like his subjects — was himself subject to the rule of the law[3]. This concept was based on the Christian idea of subjection to natural law as the supreme norm, being of divine origin. This same imitation of pontifical practice was later at the core of the emergence of the State in the secular domain, imitating the pontifical practice: the Norman reign of Sicily under Roger II, the England of Henry II, and the France of Philip Augustus[4]. For this reason it has been affirmed that the new Gregorian concept of the Church virtually demanded the invention of the concept

---

[3] See J.R. Strayer, *On the Medieval Origins of the Modern State* (Princeton, 1970), 21.

[4] See H.J. Berman, *Law and Revolution*, 89 et seq., 276 et seq. and 527 et seq. The central idea of Berman's excellent monograph is that the Gregorian Reform was the first and most important of the "revolutions" which contributed to moulding the western juridical culture.

of the State[5]. As Maitland asserted a century ago, it is impossible to frame any acceptable definition of the State which would not include the medieval Church[6].

Gierke set forth in detail the political continuity between the Middle Ages and the Modern Age, demonstrating that most of the characteristics of the modern State were already present in an embryonic stage in medieval institutions — for example, the ideas of organization, popular sovereignty and representation; or the concept of the State as a legal person subordinated to the law[7]. It is true that thinkers and rulers of the Modern Age created a new system. But, to a great extent, their task consisted in modifying pre-existing medieval ideas and adapting them to a new historical context, taking advantage of the new climate that grew out of various circumstances — principally, the decline of the empire with the growth of national monarchies, the transformation of the papacy, and the break-up of Europe's religious unity.

Modern constitutional thought did not need to renounce a medieval heritage that had been constructed within the canonical legal environment; on the contrary, it knew how to assimilate that heritage and give it a new dimension. This was possible because medieval canonists and romanists accurately perceived the central question and attempted to give it an answer — how to reconcile the concept of sovereignty with the idea of limited government, of government subject to the rule of law[8].

---

[5] J.R. Strayer, *On the Medieval Origins of the Modern State*, 22.

[6] The phrase is quoted by H.J. Berman, *Law and Revolution*, 113.

[7] See O. Gierke, *Political Theories of the Middle Age* (Cambridge, 1958; reprint of the 1st English edition, 1900). Notwithstanding that it is a century old, Gierke's analysis has continued to inspire, to a large extent, the scholars who have subsequently dealt with this subject. The extensive introduction by Maitland, who prepared the translation from the original German version, is certainly suggestive.

[8] See B. Tierney, "Medieval Law and Western Constitutionalism", within his collection of articles published under the title of *Church, Law and*

Something similar can be said with regard to the individual rights. There is a tendency to think that the western rights tradition dates back to the seventeenth century, and that its starting point was the individualist thinking of Thomas Hobbes and John Locke (although the remote roots of these two philosophers can be found in the ideas of William of Ockham). However, as Reid has recently noted, the concept of legal rights is not an entirely modern invention. Rather, it was essential to the functioning of medieval canon law, and it included — above all in matrimonial matters — an operative concept of due process. We must not underestimate the leading role that Ockham, Hobbes and Locke played in this area, but they should be seen as part of a larger tradition to which each adapted and creatively responded[9].

In a similar fashion, medieval intellectuals were greatly influenced by Greek and Roman culture, but they did not limit themselves to reiterating inherited ideas. As Tierney has shown, their originality consisted in reshaping the ideas of the ancient world in accordance with their conception of the Christian spirit, thus creating a peculiar theoretical mesh of ideas which would serve as the basis for subsequent constitutional development[10].

Constitutional Thought in the Middle Ages (London, 1979). In regard to the political doctrine of medieval canonists, see F. Calasso, *I glossatori e la teoria della sovranità* (Milano, 1957); and S. Mochi Onory, *Fonti canonistiche dell'idea moderna dello Stato* (Milano, 1951). Both Italian scholars stress that the principal contribution of the glossators in this matter consisted in realizing a juridical analysis of political problems, and this is something which gave their ideas a particular consistency. For example, Azo, the great medieval civilian, elaborated his concept of political sovereignty based on the Roman legal notion of *iurisdictio*, underlining at the same time that the source of sovereignty originates in the community. See M.P. Gilmore, *Argument from Roman law in Political Thought, 1200-1600* (Cambridge, Mass., 1941); J.W. Perrin, "Azo, Roman Law, and Sovereign European States", in *Studia Gratiana* 92 et seq. (1972).

[9] C.J. Reid, "The Canonistic Contribution to the Western Rights Tradition: An Historical Inquiry", 33 *Boston College Law Review* 37 et seq. (1991).

[10] See B. Tierney, , *Religion, Law, and the Growth of Constitutional Thought, 1150-1650* (Cambridge, 1982), 12.

This occurred because the work of medieval scholars did not remain in the ethereal sphere of academic speculation, but rather reflected the political realities of the time. The incorporation of scholarly ideas into the political realm frequently took place through a characteristic process in three phases: canon law first incorporated an institution of Roman private law, which then would be transformed into a principle of constitutional law within the ecclesiastical framework; and finally from there in its new form, it would be absorbed into the sphere of secular power[11].

Despite the singularity of English constitutional evolution, it is difficult to think that England remained entirely impervious to canonical influence. In fact, it was an English bishop, John of Salisbury, who first introduced into European thought an organic theory regarding the secular political order; he might be considered the founder of western political science[12]. The kingdom of England belonged to the same cultural and social universe as did continental monarchies, and it often played a decisive role in the European political scenario. Moreover, the Church probably possessed in the British Isles greater strength and larger jurisdictional boundaries than on the Continent. Strayer's remark in relation to the generality of western kingdoms of the

---

[11] Ibid., 25 et seq. Tierney clarifies that such a process of assimilation did not imply that European monarchs had an explicit intention of imitating the guidelines suggested by canon law. That phenomenon of mimicry occurred principally because the different persons involved — ecclesiastics and laymen — fed on the same body of juridical doctrines which proved useful and efficient. It must be remembered that the *ius commune* was born within the medieval society, where the boundaries between the temporal and spiritual environments often blurred.

[12] H.J. Berman, *Law and Revolution*, 276 et seq. The original Latin version of John of Salisbury's treatise, titled *Policraticus* and written in 1159, can be found in the edition of C.C. Webb, (Oxford,1909). There is an English translation, edited by J. Dickinson (New York, 1963). John of Salisbury was born in England in 1115, studied in Chartres for twelve years with Abelard and Gilbert de la Porrée, and served in the pontifical court at the end of the 1140s. Later, he was Thomas Becket's collaborator (actually the treatise is dedicated to him). He was bishop of Chartres from 1176 until his death, in 1180.

Middle Ages, therefore, is applicable to England: "the fact that churchmen were deeply involved in secular politics, that no ruler could function without their advice and assistance, meant that the political theories and the administrative techniques of the Church had a direct impact on lay government"[13].

And it is again Strayer who pointed out another example of ecclesiastical influence on the institutional foundations of the State. The Church contended that doing justice was one of the sovereign's essential attributes, and therefore obliged him to accept this responsibility under oath at the coronation ceremony. This idea served to reinforce the monarch's authority, and hence indirectly also favored the early establishment of effective royal courts in England[14]. It was actually a consequence of the medieval formulation of the political doctrine known as "Christian dualism" — the Church and the secular power have separate fields of competence, spiritual and temporal (although, in case of conflict, secular power must remain subordinate to the spiritual power, which was considered the superior of the two). Thus, as the ecclesiastical power became established, it contributed indirectly to strengthen the power of the King, who had the responsibility for imposing peace and justice within his kingdom.

For the rest, the existence of a Christian and canonical basis at the root of English institutions has long been recognized. Elsewhere in this essay, I cited Plucknett as noting that the medieval idea of law was accepted within the British Isles — a law that was divine in its origin, supreme in its authority, rendering justly to every man his due[15]. This same historian has also shown that in England, for a time, another principle typical of canon law was in force — the last word in the interpretation of the law strictly belongs to the legislator who promulgated it, and not to the judges[16]. After the middle of the

---

[13] J.R. Strayer, *On the Medieval Origins of the Modern State* ,16.

[14] Ibid., 31 et seq.

[15] T.F.T. Plucknett, *Concise History*, 40.

[16] Ibid., 328 et seq. Plucknett cites various cases where the King imposed his authority, by his own initiative, or even at the judges' request. One of these

fourteenth century, practice seems to have moved the other way, and statutory interpretation was relinquished to the courts, but the canonical principle did not lose its influence completely until the seventeenth century[17].

Earlier, Roscoe Pound called attention to the canonical aspect originally present in the principle of the supremacy of law. This fact is important, considering that this principle, along with the doctrine of judicial precedent — *stare decisis* — and trial by jury, constitutes one of the most distinctive features of Anglo-American legal tradition. The

---

cases occurred in 1226: in view of a certain dispute on the interpretation of *Magna Carta* between some sheriffs and the inhabitants of their shires, Henry III called the litigants before him to clear the matter up himself. The same procedure was followed eight years later, when the greater part of the bishops, earls and barons placed an interpretation upon clause 35 of *Magna Carta*, which the King then published by letters close. In 1259, Henry III wrote a warning to the Bishop of Durham, to let him know that "the interpretation of laws and customs belongs to us and our nobles, and none other". Edward I adopted a similar attitude — in 1278, the King and his judges published an extra-judicial "exposition" of the Statute of Gloucester; and in 1281, the King in Council made a "correction" of the same statute. The recourse to the legislator did not always come from the King; sometimes the common law courts themselves acknowledged the principle of appealing to the legislator when faced with difficulties of interpretation. Thus, in 1303 Chief Justice Hengham turned to the King's council to put end to a discussion, and Chief Justice Thorpe did the same in 1366.

[17] Indeed, in the seventeenth century the Chancellors Lord Ellesmere and Lord Nottingham maintained that it would be more reasonable for statutes to be interpreted by Parliament, which enacted them, than by the courts. In Plucknett's opinion, the triumph of judicial interpretation was caused principally by the historical evolution of the English Parliament: it served as a political assembly and not only as a legislature; moreover, its sessions were too irregular and its activities too much engaged in other directions to allow it to become a permanent organ for the interpretation of statutes. Even so, Plucknett identifies a remnant of the canonical principle in the creation of certain special bodies for the application of determined laws; the clearest case is the Court of the Star Chamber, in the field of criminal law (see T.F.T. Plucknett, *Concise History*, 330 et seq.).

principle of the supremacy of law can be observed consistently in the attitude and practice of English courts, which rejected subjection to the King, the legislature or the electorate; they only admitted being bound by God and the natural law. Although this principle has connections with the Germanic tradition, affirmed Pound, it was reinforced by the medieval distinction between spiritual and temporal power, which held that there is a universal law above all human authority, so that if the acts of the sovereign or Parliament run counter to this fundamental law, they must be disregarded[18].

2. Exercise of Power and Political Representation

Moving now from the level of constitutional principle to more specific points, the influence of medieval canonical doctrines can be clearly seen in two fields: the theory and practice of political representation, and the exercise of political power.

As far as the latter is concerned, the interest of canonists focused on the analysis of the supreme power (*suprema potestas*) of the Pope, not so much considered in itself, but rather in relation to the power of the community. And, trying to test the consequences of their legal solutions, canonists reflected on the possibility that the person holding the pontifical office might abuse his authority. This approach posed immediately two questions.

First, there were the relations between the pontiff and the ecumenical council. Decretists were inclined to tilt the balance in favor of the council, which seemed more secure and, above all, offered the guarantee of truly representing the community of believers; this argument would later be utilized in the conciliarist theories of the fifteenth century. Moreover, canonists emphasized that the authority of the Roman pontiff was reinforced when papal power was exercised

---

[18] See R. Pound, *The Spirit of the Common Law*, 64 et seq. In a similar direction, Calasso has remarked that the subjection of the human law to the divine law is the idea dominating the entire conception of law present in the medieval world (see F. Calasso, *Medio Evo del Diritto*, 324 et seq.).

together with that of a general council. This doctrine was subsequently echoed in the principle that the power of the King-in-Parliament was always superior to the power possessed by the King acting without Parliament[19].

The second question regarded the limits of the pontiff's *potestas* in the hypothesis that the Pope fell into heresy. It was clear that, the Pope's power being supreme, no one stood above him who was entitled to depose him from office. But, at the same time, it is an intolerable contradiction to accept a person who is simultaneously a heretic and the head of the Church. Certainly, it was not easy to reconcile the supreme authority of papacy with the need to find a remedy for that case. Finally, the canonists proposed a way to resolve the dilemma. They maintained that the community may decide the case in a "deliberative", but not in a "judicial", manner. That is to say, if the Church judged the Pope guilty of obstinate heresy, his deposition would come about automatically, *ipso iure* — by the action of the law itself, and not by virtue of any human decision.

Some centuries later, Pufendorf would argue that a similar solution should be applied in the case of a sovereign who violated the essential rules of his office. And, during the same epoch, English political life experienced a practical application of that doctrine, when in 1688 Parliament deposed James II, alleging a fictitious abdication — the monarch was said to have renounced his throne, and the members of Parliament had but recognized the fact[20].

That was not the first time a canonical doctrine had served as backcloth to the deposition of a King in England. Prior to it we find the case in which Richard II was deposed in favor of Henry IV, in 1399, because the crimes he had committed rendered him unworthy to remain on the throne[21]. There exists a valuable testimony on the subject: the

---

[19] See B. Tierney, *Religion, Law, and the Growth of Constitutional Thought*, 13 et seq.

[20] See ibid., 18 et seq.

[21] See in this respect G.E. Caspary, "The Deposition of Richard II and the Canon Law", in S. Kuttner / J.J. Ryan, eds, *Proceedings of the Second*

report written out by Adam of Usk, member of the commission of "certos doctores, episcopos et alios" (Doctors, Bishops, and others) appointed by Henry of Lancaster to study the legal grounds that could be used to justify the deposition of Richard. In his account, Adam of Usk refers explicitly to the *Ad Apostolicae dignitatis* chapter of *Liber Sextus*[22], which contains an abridged version of the sentence of deposition pronounced by Innocence IV against Emperor Frederick II in 1245. If we compare both texts, his reference appears far from merely ornamental; quite the contrary, it shows that its author had a comprehensive knowledge of the canonical document, as one would expect from the qualification as a canonist which Adam of Usk, as well as most of the bishops who took part in the legal aspects of the deposition, possessed.

Naturally, canon law was not the instrument that made the fall of Richard possible. It was simply utilized as the legal foundation for a political decision. And it did not even serve to resolve the main constitutional question involved, i.e. whether the subjects had the right to depose their King, for the canonists themselves were in dispute over the matter. It is revealing that Richard II was forced to abdicate at the same time as he was deposed, to avoid having to give a definite answer to that question[23]. In this regard, it should be borne in mind that in England the idea that the King was subject to the laws was deeply rooted, but he was not responsible to any human authority — nobody was above him —; he was responsible only to God. This was an idea

---

International Congress of Medieval Canon Law (E Civitate Vaticana, 1965), 189 et seq.; and C. Donahue, Jr., "Ius commune, Canon Law, and Common Law in England", 66 *Tulane Law Review*"1760 et seq. (1992). Regarding the deposition of Richard II in general, see M.V. Clarke And V.H. Galbraith, "The Deposition of Richard II", 14 *Bulletin of the John Rylands Lybrary* 125 et seq. (1930); and B. Wilkinson, "The Deposition of Richard II and the Accession of Henry IV", in E.B. Fryde / E. Miller, eds, *Historical Studies of the English Parliament*, vol. 1 (Cambridge, 1970), 329 et seq.

[22] *Sext.*, 2.14.2.

[23] See, in this regard, the observations of G.E. Caspary, *The Deposition of Richard II and the Canon Law*, 200 et seq.

notably propagated by Bracton, inspired by the gloss that legists and canonists had given to the rule *princeps legibus solutus est*, contained in the Digest[24]. In any case, it is interesting to note that canon law not only provided the terminology used for the deposition, but also the theoretical justification — the tyrannical behavior of the ruler — for an intervention that penetrated to the very heart of constitutional law.

Medieval canonists and scholastics, impelled by the rediscovery of Aristotelian philosophy, studied several other questions connected with the exercise and justification of power, many of which continued to attract the attention of European constitutional thinkers much later on. At the base of their exposition we find this central issue: how is authority legitimized, and what function does the consent of the subjects fulfil in this regard.

Stress on the consent of the subjects was made, above all, by the populist doctrines concerning government of the Church that were sustained by supporters of the conciliarist theories in the fifteenth century. However, even from the thirteenth century we can perceive an interest in social will as a source of the legitimacy of power, as well as what might be called the first attempts to elaborate a theory of a mixed Constitution: a government shared by the sovereign and a collegiate body — in the ecclesiastical environment, by the Pope and the College of Cardinals. Certainly those ideas were far from constituting what we would today deem a theory of democracy, but it is possible to recognize an uninterrupted chain of thought regarding the role of popular consent in government, that runs from the decretalists through to Grotius, Hobbes and Locke, on its way passing through Nicholas of Cusa, John Gerson and the Spanish scholasticism of the sixteenth century[25].

---

[24] See G. Post, "Bracton on Kingship", 42 *Tulane Law Review* 519 et seq. (1968).

[25] See Q. Skinner, *The Foundations of Modern Political Thought*, vol. 2 (Cambridge, 1978) 174 et seq.; B. Tierney, *Religion, Law, and the Growth of Constitutional Thought*, 29-102. Skinner points out that Locke drew his inspiration from many of the ideas of Spanish scholastics, but at the same time he warns against a conception of the latter as the true creators of a democratic political theory. On the contrary, it must be remembered that part of their goal

As I said before, political representation is the other aspect of constitutional law where we find the most interesting contributions by the canonists of the classical period. These contributions related specially to the notion of *persona ficta* ("fictitious person") and the maxim *quod omnes tangit debet ab omnibus approbari* ("what touches all is to be approved by all")[26].

The concept of *persona ficta* appears for the first time in the writings of Sinibaldo Fieschi, who would later be elected Pope under the name of Innocent IV, in 1243[27]. He applied it in relation to representation of the Church's patrimony, but the concept would rapidly be extended into other legal areas, and its significance for the development of mercantile law and corporation law is well-known[28]. It is true that this idea harks back to Roman law, particularly to the figure of the *universitas personarum*. However, the notion of legal personality was actually developed by the canonists, particularly the thirteenth and fourteenth centuries. They utilized it especially to explain the entire body of the Church from a legal point of view — the Church was considered as a

was to counteract the populist notion of sovereignty — in their opinion excessive — which had been developed in the fourteenth and fifteenth centuries.

[26] An excellent exposition of this subject has been given by G. Post, *Studies in Medieval Thought. Public Law and the State, 1100-1322* (Princeton, 1964), 168-184; and by B. Tierney, *Religion, Law, and the Growth of Constitutional Thought*, 19-25.

[27] See on this subject P. Gillet, *La personalité juridique en Droit ecclésiastique spécialment chez les Décretistes et les Décretalistes et dans le Code du Droit canonique* (Malines, 1927); S. Panizo Orallo, *Persona jurídica y ficción. Estudio de la obra de Sinibaldo di Fieschi* (Pamplona, 1975). In opposition to Gillet, Panizo emphasizes the significance of Sinibaldo's notion of *persona ficta* for the subsequent development of the doctrine of legal personality.

[28] See in this regard, as far as English law is concerned, Maitland's introduction to O. Gierke's, *Political Theories of the Middle Age*, cited in note 124.

juristic person, requiring the means to express its will. Canonists applied it also to diverse ecclesiastical corporations[29].

As far as the maxim *quod omnes tangit* is concerned, it also has a Justinianic origin; in Roman law it served to require the approval of all joint guardians for acts of guardianship administration[30]. The canonists inherited the maxim through Boniface VIII's *Liber Sextus* — where it is included as the 29th *regula iuris* — and they made ample use of it. First they applied it to make possible the procedural representation of all persons affected by a lawsuit, and then they utilized it also in formulating the rules governing corporations, private as well as public. On the other hand, that maxim was interpreted according to the majority principle, to make possible the viability of decision-making by a community. This fact also reflects the Roman law source of inspiration for that canonical doctrine — particularly a provision of the Digest that affirms: "what is done publicly by a majority is held to be done by all"[31].

From those bases, canonists produced a comprehensive theory on the corporate representation — embracing both private and public law — which was subsequently echoed by the constitutional thinking and practice throughout medieval Europe, England included.

For example, they spread the idea that a community could be legitimately represented and bound by the decisions taken by a corporation acting on its behalf. The argument started with the maxim *quod omnes tangit*, interpreted in the light of the majority principle, and was developed by the canonists to defend the idea that an ecumenical council represented the whole body of the Church. It meant that the

---

[29] See H.J. Berman, *Law and Revolution*, 215 et seq.; B. Tierney, *The Foundations of the Conciliar Theory* (Cambridge, 1955), 97 et seq. It is interesting to read the observations of both authors with regard to Gierke's thesis — that the corporate law of the medieval Church was a middle point between the Germanic idea of the corporation as a natural collective person and the Roman concept of the corporation as an artificial institution.

[30] See *Cod.*, 5.59.5.

[31] *Dig.* 50.17.121.

diverse members of the ecclesiastical society were virtually represented in a general assembly. In fact, this theory had immediate practical consequences, as it is confirmed by looking at the varied composition of the Fourth Lateran council, summoned in 1215 by Innocent III. Similar reasoning would serve to explain that the English Parliament represented all inhabitants of the kingdom, with the same consequences for the persons chosen to form part of it. The first visible effects of those principles can be seen in the Parliament summoned by Edward I in 1295. In Stubbs' opinion, that practical incorporation of *quod omnes tangit* signified that a simple legal maxim was being transformed into a veritable constitutional principle[32].

Moreover, medieval canonists extracted the consequences implied in the theory of representation, and they attributed to representatives *plena potestas* ("full power") to act on behalf of the persons being represented, who thus became directly bound by the decisions adopted even if they had not specifically approved of each of them. That principle was initially applied in procedural law, referring to the acts of the person representing a corporation in a trial. Then it passed into the constitutional sphere, where it would be utilized to define the powers possessed by members elected to constitute an assembly of a representative nature.

It might be argued that application of this idea to the powers of Parliament's members might have been an inevitable consequence of England's political evolution. Yet it is significant that, in England, the idea was embraced shortly after it had been put into practice by the ecclesiastical power and, later on, by several continental kingdoms. Indeed, Pope Innocent III was the first to make use of that formula in

---

[32] Cited by Tierney, *Religion, Law, and the Growth of Constitutional Thought,* 25. A detailed exposition of how the English Parliament evolved in this regard, can be found in W. Stubbs, *The Constitutional History of England*, especially chapters V and VI. See also C. Donahue, Jr., *Ius commune, Canon Law, and Common Law*, 1754, who points out that the English Parliament, in the exercise of its judicial functions, and particularly in criminal cases, made use of ideas proceeding from the learned laws, such as the presentation of articles and proof by notoriety.

relation to an assembly of representatives from six cities of the papal states that was celebrated in 1200. Also in the ecclesiastical realm, in 1228, the members of the general Chapter of the Dominican Order possessed a mandate with *plena potestas*. Emperor Frederick II followed this example three years later, when he summoned an assembly of the representatives of Tuscan cities who were endowed with "full authority". By the end of thirteenth century, the practice had been imitated in numerous regions of Europe[33]. It is not likely to have been a pure chronological coincidence that in England the practice was adopted for the first time for the Parliament of 1268, and that the term "full power" remained invariably in the summons to Parliament that took place between 1294 and 1872.

Let us still say a word on the role played by the so-called "saniority principle" as a factor counter to the majority principle. It constitutes one of the most characteristic features of the canonical doctrine on decision-making by collegiate bodies acting in representation of a collectivity of people. The general rule was that decisions were taken according to the opinion of the majority (*maior pars*). Nevertheless, the law also adopted an effective means of checking the force of numbers. Sometimes the majority opinion was bound to yield to the position of the *sanior pars* (literally the more "sane" part, the more discerning part), i.e. the minority who held a position considered of superior worth, which corresponded more accurately with the objective rules of a dogmatic, moral or legal character[34].

Undoubtedly this situation could give rise to practical abuses, but it is no less certain that the *sanior pars* doctrine implied an affirmation of the supremacy of legal norms, to which the majority of a political assembly must also surrender. In any case, it undeniably influenced subsequent political thinking, which would resort to that principle in order to justify the authority of an assembly that acted without being

---

[33] See G. Post, *Studies in Medieval Legal Thought*, 108 et seq.; B. Tierney, *Religion, Law, and the Growth of Constitutional Thought*, 24 et seq.

[34] On the concept of *sanior pars*, see R.H. Helmholz, *The Spirit of Classical Canon Law*, 52-58.

bound by the statistical majority of the socially inferior classes. Possibly the best known historical example of it is the *valentior pars* doctrine advocated by Marsilius of Padova[35]. Some scholars have even tried to establish a historical link between the "saniority" principle and the system of checks and balances characteristic of Anglo-American constitutional practice[36].

Finally we should mention an embryonic theory of the State in the works of glossators from the late twelfth century. They supported, against imperial and papal power, the independent authority of national monarchs, as a logical consequence of every kingdom's status as a corporation (*universitas*)[37]. Or we may also cite the antecedents of the "reason of State" doctrine which an analysis of the writings of various medieval canonists, civilians and scholastics reveals[38]. It is virtually impossible to assess the exact weight that all those legal creations had on the constitutional evolution of England. However, if one admits that there is an interaction between theory and practice in this area of law, it seems undeniable that canonical contributions have been of real importance.

---

[35] See B. Tierney, *Religion, Law, and the Growth of Constitutional Thought*, 23.

[36] See S. Luppi, "Secolarizzazioni del principio sanioritario. *Sanior pars*, sovranità e limiti del potere fra cristianesimo e secolarizzazione", in L. Lombardi Vallauri / G. Dilcher, eds, *Cristianesimo, Secolarizzazione e diritto moderno* (Milano and Baden-Baden, 1981), 627 et seq.

[37] One of the first thinkers to sustain that doctrine was the English author Ricardus Anglicus. See E.F. Jacob, "Political Thought", in C.G. Crump / E.F. Jacob, eds, *The Legacy of the Middle Ages* (Oxford, 1969; reprint of the 1932 edition); B. Tierney, *Religion, Law, and the Growth of Constitutional Thought*, 21 et seq. A much more detailed analysis can be read in the already cited books of F. Calasso, *I glossatori e la teoria della sovranità*, and S. Mochi Onory, *Fonti canonistiche dell'idea moderna dello Stato.*

[38] See G. Post, *Studies in Medieval Legal Thought*, 241 et seq.

Chapter 10

Other Areas of Law

1. Procedural Law

Procedural law is normally considered as a paradigm of the areas of English law which have experienced an entirely insular development. According to this view, Anglo-American procedure was a product exclusively of practice in the common law courts, free from continental "contamination". In this regard, Van Caenegem's opinion about the reasons why England did not receive the Roman-canonical procedure, as the rest of European countries did, has been influential[1]. He argued that, when the evolution of the continental *ius commune* began to produce a workable procedural law in the late twelfth century, common law procedure was already firmly established. Consequently English lawyers felt less need than did their continental colleagues to resort to the new procedural system emerging from the universities and papal decretals.

Certainly, anyone observing how justice is administered today in Anglo-American and in continental courts realizes that there are

---

[1] See chapter 2, notes 32-33 and accompanying text; R.C. Van Caenegem, "L'histoire du Droit et la chronologie. Réflexions sur la formation du *common law* et la procédure romano-canonique", in *Études d'histoire du Droit dédiées à Gabriel Le Bras*, vol. 2, (Paris, 1965), 1459-1465.

profound differences between them[2]. Nevertheless, it is very likely that not even English procedural law remained immune to the influence of the "learned law" developed by the jurists teaching at the medieval European universities.

In fact, the imprint left by the *ius commune* on the beginnings of the procedural system of the common law has long been recognized. From a general point of view, it has long been admitted that English procedure came to be rationalized thanks to the Roman-canonical contributions. It has also been maintained that common lawyers borrowed a great part of the ideas which permitted them to develop the science of pleading, a science which was an impelling force of the entire evolution of the common law, centered in the procedural practice of the royal courts[3].

Moreover, Post emphasized the procedural significance of the maxim *quod omnes tangit debet ab omnibus approbari* ("what touches all is to be approved by all"), embraced by canon law from Roman sources, as already mentioned in the chapter on constitutional law[4]. Inspired by canonical texts, Bracton adopted this principle, and utilized it in procedural law for the same purpose that it had been applied by canonists, i.e. to demand the representation in litigation of all persons affected. In this particular, the common law courts accommodated their practice to Bracton's doctrine[5].

---

[2] It is more difficult determine which of the two procedural systems is more efficient — probably each one is the most appropriate for its own socio-juridical context. As an anecdote, I will cite the words that Merryman attributes to an academic when asked about which criminal procedure, with or without jury, seemed more just: "he said that if he were innocent, he would prefer to be tried by a civil law court, but that if he were guilty, he would prefer to be tried by a common law court" (J.H. Merryman, *The Civil Law Tradition*, 132).

[3] See H.D. Hazeltine, *Roman and Canon Law in the Middle Ages*, 758 et seq.; F. Pollock / F.W. Maitland, *History of English Law*, vol. 2, 611 et seq.

[4] See chapter 9.2.

[5] See G. Post, *Studies in Medieval Legal Thought*, 196 et seq.

Other authors have also pointed out the parallel between certain procedural institutions of canon law and common law, although there is not sufficient historical evidence to conclude beyond doubt that the latter resulted from effective canonical influence. This resemblance can be found particularly between the writs of the royal courts and the pontifical rescripts (*rescripta*) which conceded jurisdiction to the judges delegate of the Pope to try causes which had been appealed to Rome[6]. Something similar can be stated in relation to the canonical doctrine of judicial *recusatio* (recusal) — an antecedent of the right to be tried by an impartial judge, which constitutes an essential part of due process of law[7].

Anglo-American historians have also raised the question of the possible influence of canon law on the beginnings of the jury. It is presumable that ecclesiastical law contributed — at least indirectly — to the expansion of the jury as a means of proof in replacing the irrational system of ordeals[8]. The participation of the clergy in ordeals had been a regular practice before it was prohibited by the fourth Lateran Council in 1215[9]. By 1219, English law had accepted this ecclesiastical decision and was moving towards the use of juries in response. Some scholars have recently sought to minimize the

---

6 R.C. Van Caenegem, *The Birth of the English Common Law*, 59 et seq.

7 See R.H. Helmholz, "Canonists and Standards of Impartiality for Papal Judges Delegate", in *Canon Law and the Law of England*, 21 et seq. It should in any case be noted that this right does not arise in the common law until a later date: not before the sixteenth century.

8 See W.S. Holdsworth, *History of English Law*, vol. 1, 311; T.F.T. Plucknett, *Concise History*, 114 et seq.; O. Rabasa, *El derecho angloamericano*, 115; R.C. Van Caenegem, *The Birth of the English Common Law*, 62 et seq.

9 In relation to the struggle of the Church against the ordeals, see J. Gaudemet, "Les ordalies au Moyen Âge: doctrine, législation et pratique canonique", in 18 *Rec. Société Jean Bodin* 99 et seq. (Bruxelles, 1965).

significance of the Lateran decrees[10], but it is indisputable that the jury system became definitely consolidated only from the thirteenth century on, even though it had been instituted by Henry II in the middle of the previous century.

Less open to uncertainty is the influence evident in that Glanvill and Bracton took the rules relating to the examination and disqualification of jurors from the parallel rules of canon law on the selection of witnesses[11]. Likewise, significant coincidences exist between the jury regulation in the Assize of Clarendon — promulgated by Henry II in 1166 — and the *ex officio* procedure used by the English ecclesiastical courts in criminal causes. In the latter, the preliminary issue was always to ascertain, often by means of an inquest among "sworn men", the public reputation of the accused. This was the very purpose for which Henry II established the presentment jury. Moreover, although canonical procedure was more inclined to proof by witnesses, in practice the English Church courts often resorted to the so-called *purgatio canonica*. In it the accused was required to take a formal oath that he was innocent and to find a number of *compurgatores* or oath-helpers (often twelve, the same number as jury members), i.e. people willing to swear that they believed his oath of innocence was true[12]. It is controversial whether the drafters of the Clarendon rules based their

---

[10] For example, R. Bartlett, *Trial by Fire and Water* (New York, 1986), and P. Hyams, "Trial by Ordeal: The Key to Proof in the Early Common Law", in *On the Laws and Customs of England* (Chapel Hill, 1981), 90 et seq.

[11] The fact is well-known enough, and I have mentioned it supra, in chapter 5. See T.F.T. Plucknett, *Concise History*, 433, and F. Pollock / F.W. Maitland, *History of English Law*, vol. 1, 134.

[12] The canonical oaths of compurgation are well described by R.H. Helmholz, *The Spirit of Classical Canon Law*, 158-159. Helmholz affirms that it became the rule in the classical canon law that the number of compurgators required was "arbitrary", i.e. determined by the judge according to his view of the exigencies of the case.

work on that ecclesiastical experience, but it may be assumed with certainty that they did know it[13].

The subsequent evolution of the English jury followed its own course, one quite different from the path along which Roman-canonical procedure moved, centered as it was in the predominance of proof by witnesses. This divergence seems to introduce a double objection to the argument for the influence of canon law on the development of Anglo-American procedure. First, there is no historical evidence incontestable enough to assert categorically a cause and effect connection between the procedural rules of canon law and common law praxis. Second, it might be objected that most of the aforementioned points of similarity are relatively marginal, and refer to an early period, before common law procedure had established its own identity, completely independent from what was occurring in the continental legal world.

Certainly there is a substantial truth in those statements, but in my opinion they must be counterbalanced by two considerations.

First, Anglo-American law continued to absorb procedural principles from the Continent for a period longer than is commonly believed. A clear example is the privilege against self-incrimination, i.e. the right not to provide evidence against oneself, expressed in the Latin maxim *nemo tenetur prodere seipsum*. It has traditionally been considered one of the most specific creations of the English judiciary, allegedly in contrast with the positions of the continental *ius commune* and with the practice of the English ecclesiastical courts[14]. Never-

[13] See R.H. Helmholz, "The Early History of the Grand Jury and the Canon Law, 50 *University of Chicago Law Review* 613 et seq. (1983). In regard to the use of jurylike bodies by English ecclesiastical courts, see C. Donahue, Jr., *Proof by Witnesses in the Church Courts of Medieval England*, 134 et seq.; R.C. Van Caenegem, "Public Prosecution of Crime in Twelfth Century England", in *Church and Government in the Middle Ages* (Cambridge, 1976), 61 et seq. Van Caenegem definitely considers that the ecclesiastical practice was one of the important preexistent elements which inspired the creation of the jury by Henry II.

[14] Including, above all, the High Commission established by the Tudors for the prosecution of grave religious offences. The acceptance of that idea

theless, it has recently been demonstrated that the antecedents of this principle must be traced back to the medieval *ius commune* — especially to the works of the canonists — and that it arose in English law in a way that does not seem wholly alien to contemporary practice in the English Church courts[15].

The second and more important point is that Anglo-American procedure was not formed solely within the common law courts, but also from elements contributed by other jurisdictions, principally by the equitable jurisdiction. Many of the most significant features of Anglo-American procedure emerged from the unification of law and equity in nineteenth century England. The Court of Chancery's procedural practice was largely modeled on Roman-canonical rules. After unification, they introduced important elements to the common law procedure that is today in force. Among these elements are: the injunction; most forms of relief other than damages; the use of affidavits and interrogatories; trial by judge alone; examination of the parties as witnesses; the present High Court writ, which is modeled on the *subpœna* rather than the original writ of the common law. This is not to

---

gained momentum with Levy's theses (which have been explained and criticized in the work of Helmholz cited in the following note).

[15] Helmholz has noted that the principle *nemo tenet prodere seipsum* was not only utilized in ecclesiastical courts, but also appears in some of the most influential works of the Later Middle Age canonists: the ordinary gloss to Gregory IX's decretals, and the writings of Sinibaldo Fieschi and Panormitanus. Nevertheless, Helmholz remarks that the common law judges transformed into a veritable law of the person what for the continental canonists and civilians was only a mechanism of protection against an abusive interference of authority in the individuals' privacy — the *ex officio* oath, requiring defendants to swear in advance to answer truthfully any questions to be put to them by the court, among which some interrogations directed at self-incrimination were frequently included. See R.H. Helmholz, "Origins of the Privilege against Self-Incrimination: The Role of the European *Ius Commune*", 67 *New York University Law Review* 962 et seq. (1990). See also M.R.T. Macnair, "The Early Development of the Privilege against Self-Incrimination", 10 *Oxford Journal of legal Studies* 67 et seq. (1990).

mention the procedure for discovery of evidence, which entitles the judge to order the parties to produce documents in their possession[16].

2. Criminal Law

It is well known that the moral doctrine of the Catholic Church was reflected by the parallel theory and practice of the canon law on crime. The legal constructs of canon law on this matter, in turn, substantially contributed to reshaping the secular legal systems of the Occident during the Middle Ages, pushing aside some fundamental notions of Germanic origin which had spread through Europe with the expansion of the Barbarian peoples. So important was this ecclesiastical influence that canon law has eloquently been labeled as "a source of the ancient secular criminal law"[17].

An interesting example of the canonical imprint on secular criminal law is the twelfth century doctrine of Peter Lombard according to which "there is no sin where there was no prohibition"[18]. Some centuries later, this theological principle would be rediscovered by the penal law, and expressed in the maxim *nullum crimen, nulla pœna sine lege* (no crime, no punishment without a law)[19].

According to Berman, there was another theological principle at work, the eleventh century doctrine of Saint Anselm on atonement. It had a powerful influence on the retributive theory of justice which inspired western criminal law during the following centuries. The

---

[16] See J.H. Baker, *An Introduction to English Legal History*, 96-97.

[17] A. Laingui, "Le droit pénal canonique, source de l'ancien droit pénal laic", in *Églises et pouvoir politique* (Angers, 1987), 213 et seq. See also J.M. Carrasse, in "L'influence de la Bible sur l'ancien droit pénal francais (XII-XVIII siècles)", 35 *L'année canonique* 103 et seq. (1992).

[18] "Non enim consisteret peccatum, si interdictio non fuisset", Peter Lombard, *Sententiarum Libri Quatuor*, Migne, *PL* 192.734 (quoted by Berman, see following note).

[19] H.J. Berman, *Law and Revolution*, 186 et seq., who emphasizes the use of the past tense — "was" — in the sentence of Peter Lombard.

central idea was that the divine order of the universe required the penitence of the sinner and his punishment when he had transgressed against the law. Consequently, when a crime was committed, the most important thing was not so much to avenge the honor of the victim or to remedy his social loss, but rather to repair the violation of the law itself[20].

In sum, moral concepts were transplanted into the legal world, so that a criminal was considered above all as a sinner. For this reason, the fundamental contributions of medieval Christian theology to western criminal law go beyond introducing the idea of retribution. They also include two important elements: the concept of delinquent's rehabilitation that is necessary to make his eternal salvation possible; and the notion of subjective guilt as an integral element of crime.

Concerning the former, the Church introduced a new dimension in the concept of incarceration. As applied by the temporal power, it was originally a purely preventive measure. But canon law conceded a special significance to the rehabilitative aspect of the penal sanction, and not only to its retributive aim. The natural consequence was the use of incarceration as a punitive measure, and a mitigation of the cruel corporal punishments of the Middle Ages, while at the same time the authorities endeavored to induce the criminal's repentance through the contemplation promoted by solitary confinement[21].

The second element is more important, however, for it concerns the very roots of criminal law — the progressive transformation of criminal responsibility into a more subjective concept, which was established by canon law in contrast with the Germanic notion of purely objective responsibility. As I have just mentioned, the starting point of ecclesiastical doctrine was that the crime had to be judged from the

---

[20] Ibid. 174 et seq. Berman compares this doctrine with a meaningful phrase of Justice Oliver Wendell Holmes, referring to what he would say to a criminal about to be executed: "The law must keep its promises" (Ibid., 185 and note 42).

[21] See G. Le Bras, "Canon Law", in C.G. Crump / E.F. Jacobs Eds, *The legacy of the middle Ages*, 357 et seq.

perspective of sin. This meant that subjective guilt was an essential factor of any crime to be punishable. Consequently, the focus shifted from the crime to the criminal, and the intentional element of the crime had to be considered in order to impose criminal sanctions. Such was the requirement expressed by the 23rd *regula iuris* of the *Liber Sextus* of Pope Boniface VIII: "*sine culpa, nisi subsit causa, non est aliquis puniendus*". This idea, which had its origin in moral theology, passed later to the legal environment and was technically advanced by resorting to the Roman law notions of *dolus* (fraud) and *culpa* (guilt)[22].

The expansion of classical canon law meant that this mesh of fundamental ideas ended up by reshaping the nature of criminal law in western legal systems. In the Continent, this influence naturally came about through the *ius commune*. England also experienced the impact of those new canonical ideas, but through different channels.

The ecclesiastical penitential system had begun to pervade the British Isles long before the Norman Conquest, mainly by means of the so-called *libri pœnitentiales* or "penitential books" — catalogues of moral offences with corresponding sanctions, which became enormously widespread in Great Britain and in Ireland[23]. So long lived was the ecclesiastical influence that, even in the seventeenth century, it reached the Court of Star Chamber, one of the supreme royal courts with competence over several specific offences, which incorporated some significant elements into the English criminal law[24].

---

[22] See F. Pollock / W. Maitland, *History of English Law*, vol. 2, 474 et seq.

[23] Although the golden age of penitential books in England occurred before the birth of the common law, it is presumable that their influence would extend beyond the times of the Norman Conquest, especially in relation to the moral convictions which constituted the foundations for the development of criminal law. See T.P. Oakley, *English Penitential Discipline and Anglo-Saxon Law in their Joint Influence* (New York, 1969; reprint of the 1923 ed).

[24] See R. Pound, *The Spirit of the Common Law*, 50 et seq. With regard to the role played by the Star Chamber in English law, see S.F.C. Milsom, *Historical Foundations*, 417 et seq. The Court of Star Chamber was

In any event, the largest contingent of canonical notions of criminal law entered England during the centuries following the Conquest. Throughout the later Middle Ages, the English ecclesiastical courts exercised an extensive jurisdiction on criminal matters. The Crown sometimes opposed strongly[25], sometimes supported, and sometimes remained indifferent to it.

That jurisdiction was at times exercised on issues in which the Church possessed a direct interest: especially causes where clergymen were involved, offences relating to sacred places, and cases where a secular crime arose incidentally during proceedings before an ecclesiastical judge. In addition, as a consequence of the ecclesiastical jurisdiction on marriage, the Church exercised a virtually undisputed jurisdiction over sexual offences (adultery, fornication, incest)[26]. In a similar way, English legal life witnessed a jurisdictional expansion of the Church courts — often caused by the need to fill the practical voids of the common law — to reach certain conduct society tended then to judge from a moral point of view rather than from a purely legal perspective: perjury, usury or infanticide, for example[27].

---

established at the beginning of the sixteenth century, and abolished in the middle of the seventeenth century. However, many of its constructs became incorporated permanently in the common law. Its peculiar name, it seems, comes from the gilded stars that adorned the ceiling of the room where the court used to meet.

[25] The most famous case is the struggle between Henry II and Thomas Becket, in the twelfth century, with regard to the *privilegium fori* or benefit of clergy: a canonical institution aimed at safeguarding the exclusive competence of ecclesiastical jurisdiction over crimes committed by clergymen. As it is well-known, the struggle acquired a particular slant when Becket was murdered in Canterbury Cathedral: that event provoked sufficient pressure to move the King to make important concessions on this matter. See L. Gabel, *Benefit of the Clergy in England in the Latter Middle Ages* (Northampton, 1929).

[26] I have already mentioned this fact in chapter 6.2.

[27] With regard to the criminal jurisdiction of ecclesiastical courts generally, see the different treatises on the history of English law repeatedly

It is undeniable that aspects of canonical thought have left an enduring imprint upon the general principles governing English criminal law. But ecclesiastical influence is also identifiable in the specific legal regulation of certain offences. For example, Scrutton took note of one in the principle of the collective liability impose upon the people intervening in a fray. According to this rule the damage caused by one must be imputed to all; this principle was introduced into English law by Bracton, who took it from a papal decretal directed to Thomas Becket[28]. Another example is provided by Baker, who is of the opinion that the ecclesiastical notion of infamy — exemplified by the form of the sentence of anathema — may have contributed to strengthen the idea that "corruption of the blood" should follow conviction of a serious crime, which in turn became an inspiration for the legal treatment of felony. Indeed, in English law, felony was treated as a fundamental breach of the contract of homage, in such a way that the felon forfeited his holding, and his children were deprived of their right to inherit the felon's property. This rule remained in force until 1870[29].

However, the clearest case of canonical influence is probably the common law on defamation, which experienced a long and complex process of sedimentation. For many years, British and American historians have realized how important the canonical element had been in that evolution[30]. Modern Anglo-American historiography has

---

cited in this book. In relation to more specific aspects, the information and analysis contained in some of the works of R.H. Helmholz is very useful; see especially his articles "Crime, Compurgation and the Courts of the Medieval Church" and "Infanticide in the Province of Canterbury during the Fifteenth Century", both included in his book *Canon Law and the Law of England*, 119 et seq., and 157 et seq. Regarding infanticide, see also B.A. Kellum, "Infanticide in England in the Later Middle Ages", 1 *History of Childhood Quarterly* 371 et seq. (1974).

[28] T.E. Scrutton, *The Influence of the Roman Law*, 108.

[29] J.H. Baker, *An Introduction to English Legal History*, 412 et seq.

[30] See F. Pollock / F.W. Maitland, *History of English Law*, vol. 2, 536 et seq.; T.F.T. Plucknett, *Concise History*, 483 et seq.; V.V. Veeder, "The

continued to study the subject and, despite numerous questions that are still unanswered, there are also conclusions of remarkable interest[31].

At least from the thirteenth century, the English ecclesiastical courts exercised an effective and almost exclusive jurisdiction over defamation. Indeed, the 1286 statute *Circumspecte agatis* sought to limit the activity of the Church courts: they were prohibited from granting compensatory damages to the injured party. This prohibition, however, proved to have only limited effect[32]. The Church courts followed some Roman law principles in their decisions up to a certain extent, but in most respects applied a system of their own[33]. Rather than the expansive *actio iniuriarum* of Roman law, the ecclesiastical courts enforced a more restricted version of defamation. This was understood as the malicious imputation of a crime, excluding language which we

History of the Law of Defamation", in *Select Essays in Anglo-American Legal History*, vol. 3, 446 et seq.

[31] The most extensive study of this subject has been made by R.H. Helmholz, introduction to *Select Cases on Defamation to 1600* (London: Selden Society, 1985). See also J.L. Barton, *Roman Law in England*, 93 et seq.; R.H. Helmholz, "Canonical Defamation in Medieval England", 15 *American Journal of Legal History*, 255 et seq. (1971), and by the same author, "Canon Law and the English Common Law", in *Canon law and the law of England*, 8 et seq.; S.F.C. Milsom, *Historical Foundations*, 380 et seq.

[32] Milsom has pointed out that nothing prevented the Church from mitigating the offender's punishment if he agreed to compensate the offended person. That solution was often utilized in practice, and constituted an indirect way of conceding compensatory damages in the ecclesiastical forum, consequently outwitting the *Circumspecte agatis* prohibition. On the other hand, Milsom specifies that the *Circumspecte agatis*, was not actually a statute, but rather a writing containing some directions for the judges of the Crown (S.F.C. Milsom, *Historical Foundations*, 381).

[33] Sometimes, a peculiar penitence was imposed in cases of defamation: the culprit had to recognize publicly that his statement was false, and had also to implore the pardon of the offended, all in the presence of the Parish priests. It is interesting to observe that Bentham, some centuries later, would propose a similar punishment for defamation. See F. Carr, "The English Law of Defamation", 18 *Law Quarterly Review* 272 (1902).

today take to be slanderous — like imputations of professional unfitness — as well as mere abusive language.

The common law courts actually began to hear defamation cases only during the sixteenth century. From the beginning, common lawyers followed many of the guidelines laid out in ecclesiastical jurisdiction, on procedural as well as on substantive issues. Until the very end of the 1500's, the conduct that common law courts qualified as defamation corresponded to the restricted concept of canon law. For instance, the *mitior sensus* rule, adopted by the common lawyers, according to which words would be given a lenient, non-actionable interpretation if this were possible, was in fact simply a rigorous application of the canonical rule that to be actionable, the defamatory words must tend to subject the victim to criminal prosecution[34]. Thereafter the common law, though partly influenced by canonical precedents and partly impelled by doctrines of Star Chamber, followed its own course in constructing the legal regulation of libel and slander[35]. Yet the influence of ecclesiastical courts did not wholly disappear, as in treating malice as an integral element of those crimes.

3. Real Property Law

If there is a branch of the common law with the aura of absolute isolation from continental law, it is the land law. There is much truth to this view, and it is natural that it should have been so, as the royal courts concentrated their efforts and creativity in this area of law, from the very outset of the judicial system organized under the Norman and Angevin kings.

---

[34] R.H. Helmholz, *Canon Law and English Common Law*, 10.

[35] A fundamental milestone on that path was the well-known *De libellis famosis* case in 1609, reported by Sir Edward Coke in his *Reports*: see the edition of Fraser and Thomas, vol. 3 (London, 1826), 254 et seq. Libel is defamation expressed by print, writing, pictures, or signs. Slander is oral defamation.

However, it is not likely that the English law of real property could develop in total isolation, because, among other reasons, development of that aspect of English law did not proceed exclusively from the common law courts. Furthermore, the common law itself does not appear to have evolved wholly without contact with the legal constructs of medieval canon law. Indeed, the ecclesiastical courts had an indirect influence at least on two aspects of English real estate law during the Middle Ages.

One has been mentioned before: the Church courts could exercise jurisdiction over testaments only in respect to chattels, since this was the only kind of property that could be freely bequeathed by the testator. This fact accentuated, as a side effect, the conceptual and jurisdictional differentiation between the two classes of property, personal and real, reserving the latter for the exclusive competence of the common law courts. As Maitland put it, ecclesiastical jurisdiction over testament "had the effect of splitting our English law of property into two halves"[36].

The second occurred with an institution which emerged in the twelfth century: the leasehold or *term of years*. Maitland himself affirmed that the imprint of Roman law was noticeable in it, saying that it might be deemed a sort of usufruct[37]. Joüon des Longrais, however, thought that the term of years had no connection with Roman law; its the purpose was to elude ecclesiastical prohibitions against usury. Its principal aim was to render the lending of money at a high interest possible, by using land as security. The lender typically loaned a sum of money to a landowner in financial difficulties. In exchange, the lender obtained possession of the land for a period long enough to recover both capital and interest through the rents of the land[38].

In addition to these possible examples of indirect influence, there has also been some clearer direct influence of canon law on the English

---

[36] F. Pollock / F.W. Maitland, *History of English Law*, vol. 1, 128.

[37] F. Pollock / F.W. Maitland, *History of English Law*, vol. 2, 114 et seq.

[38] See F. Joüon des Longrais, *La conception anglaise de la saisine* (Paris, 1925), 141 et seq.

law of real property. Among these, the subject most discussed by historians is whether the so-called assize of *novel disseisin*, created by Henry II in 1166, was inspired by canon law. This assize provided a procedure by which a person who had been dispossessed of his land was entitled to recover it immediately. Only when the initial situation had been restored, could judicial proceedings to determine which of the contenders had the better title to the property commence.

More than a century ago, Scrutton suggested that the assize of novel disseisin might have been built on Roman and canonical foundations[39]. Maitland echoed Scrutton's suggestion, and adding that the novel disseisin's origin was probably the *actio spolii* of canon law, an action which was in turn founded upon the possessory interdict *unde vi* of Roman law[40]. Vinogradoff accepted this fact as indubitable[41]. Some years later, Woodbine enlarged those conclusions, claiming that the action of trespass — a more extensive remedy against intrusions on real property — also had canonical roots, running through the influence the *actio spolii* had on the assize of novel disseisin[42].

Subsequently, Plucknett — inspired by Joüon des Longrais — adopted a more skeptical attitude about the possibility of canonical influence, maintaining that the assize established by Henry II was so obviously reasonable that it is unnecessary to search for any canonical antecedents[43]. Still more emphatically, Richardson, Sayles and Van Caenegem have denied the Roman or canonical origin of that action, making two principal arguments. First, the assize of novel disseisin precedes the *actio spolii* chronologically. And second, a comparative

---

[39] T.E. Scrutton, *The Influence of the Roman Law*, 112 et seq.

[40] F. Pollock / F.W. Maitland, *History of English Law*, vol. 2, 47 et seq.

[41] P. Vinogradoff, *Roman Law in Medieval Europe*, 99.

[42] G.E. Woodbine, "The Origins of the Action of Trespass", 33*Yale Law Journal* 799 et seq. (1924), and 34 *Yale Law Journal* 343 et seq. (1925). Woodbine, as most Anglo-American historians later did, based his conclusions on the book of F. Ruffini, *L'actio spolii* (Torino, 1889).

[43] T.F.T. Plucknett, *Concise History*, 359.

analysis of the common law remedy and parallel features of Roman and canon law discloses significant differences between them; especially, the latter were possessory actions, preliminary to the discussion over property rights, while novel disseisin, though beginning as a purely possessory action, in fact almost always definitely decided the issue of the title[44]. More recently, Sutherland has revisited the matter in a deep investigation, and although he considers the canonical influence more doubtful, he is inclined to accept a romanistic inspiration for novel disseisin, as well as for the *actio spolii*[45].

It is not my intention to join in the debate regarding the history of this action, which declines from the beginning of the sixteenth century, and completely disappears by the middle of the seventeenth century. However, it is my hope that several points will help to put the conclusions reached by other historians into exact perspective.

First, in my opinion little significance should be conceded to the chronological factor in order to deny the possible canonical origin of novel disseisin. It is true that — under a different name — the *actio spolii* does not emerge as an effective action until the end of the twelfth century. But Le Bras has demonstrated that the principle *spoliatus ante omnia restituendus* (before anything else is done, the dispossessed person has the right to restitution) was operative in canon law from the ninth century, being employed as a procedural remedy in the case of bishops who had been stripped of their property. In the eleventh century, that remedy was often utilized in favor of others, even sometimes when dispossession had been only partial. These older precedents were the foundations on which a veritable possessory action

---

[44] See H.G. Richardson / G.O. Sayles, *Introduction to Select Cases of Procedure without Writ* (London: Selden Society, 1941), cviii et seq. and cxxviii et seq.; R.C. Van Caenegem, *Royal Writs in England from the Conquest to Glanvill*, 386 et seq., and *The Birth of the English Common Law*, 44. Van Caenegem is inclined to think that the assize of novel disseisin had Germanic roots.

[45] D.W. Sutherland, *The Assize of Novel Disseisin* (Oxford, 1973), 20 et seq.

was subsequently construed[46]. Therefore, by the time the assize of novel disseisin was created, the principle of the *restitutio spolii* already had a canonical pedigree, and was itself quite well known in England.

Furthermore, other relevant data counsel us not to discard the possibility that canon law — rather than Roman law — influenced the birth and development of novel disseisin. The canonical concept of possessory remedies was wider than the parallel interdict of Roman law; canon law applied them to other types of *deiectio* (dispossession) than those accomplished through violence, and this was also a feature characteristic of novel disseisin. Moreover, contrary to the Roman interdict *unde vi*, the assize of novel disseisin also served to protect forms of possession beyond that of physical possession of land (for example, the rights of common grazing for cattle). We should bear in mind that legal historians have long noted the influence of canon law on the beginnings of the common law relating to the possession of incorporeal goods[47].

Second, quite apart from direct canonical influence on the common law, it is indubitable that the English law of property was significantly shaped by the actions of the Court of Chancery, in all likelihood in ways that were connected with the doctrine and practice of the canon law of the time. This occurred principally in two areas: the mortgage and the law of uses.

In regard to the mortgage, the original common law was particularly strict against the debtor; if there were any delay in repaying the loan, the creditor obtained the right to the mortgaged land[48]. This result, moreover, appears to have been widespread throughout medieval

---

[46] See G. Le Bras, "Canon Law", in C.G. Crump / E.F. Jacobs Eds, *The Legacy of the Middle Ages*, 350 et seq. The French historian explains that the action against dispossession appears for the first time in the *Summa* of Sicardus of Cremona, around the year 1180, under the name of *condictio ex canone redintegranda*.

[47] See H.J. Berman, *Law and Revolution*, 240 et seq.; F. Pollock / F.W. Maitland, *History of English Law*, vol. 2, 135 et seq.

[48] The same rule was applied in case of pledge of personal property.

Europe. The Church, however, considered it abusive and declared its opposition to it openly in the third Lateran Council, in 1178. By the fourteenth century, Chancery had managed to intervene in favor of the debtor, acting on equitable principles that implied protecting people against damage unjustly suffered and treating a mortgage as only surety. The doctrine that inspired Chancery's action was substantially the same as the idea expressed two centuries before by the third Lateran Council. When the payment of the loan was delayed, the mortgage was considered to be subject to an equitable right to redeem it, so that the debtor did not lose the property of the land mortgaged; it simply served as a guarantee that the sum borrowed would be paid to the creditor. By Charles I's time, the principle of the equity of redemption in mortgages in equity was thoroughly established in England[49].

The use is the ancestor of the trust, and is well-known to legal historians. Therefore, it is not necessary to enter into a detailed explanation of its evolution and characteristics. Suffice it to say that this institution emerged as a peculiar way of transferring property with the purpose of evading some of the more rigid rules of the common law. In short, the use required that property be conveyed to a certain person for a beneficiary, who could not himself be appointed the legal owner but who obtained the actual beneficial enjoyment of the land transferred. In other words, the land was legally transmitted to a determined person, but *ad opus* (to the use or benefit) of another person.

The common law recognized only the legal owner, who was morally but not legally, obliged to act in accordance with the trust reposed in him. Thus the whole relationship created by the use was founded on confidence, so that if the person holding legal ownership (*feoffee*) violated his duty, the beneficiary (*cestui que use*) remained unprotected by the common law. However, this moral obligation came to be judicially enforceable in Chancery, which, being a court of conscience, could intervene in these conflicts between strict law and moral duties. At least from the fourteenth century, the Chancellors regularly exercised their jurisdiction over uses, to such an extent that a new form

---

[49] See G. Spence, *Equitable Jurisdiction*, vol. 1, 599 et seq.; J.D. Davies, "Equity in English Law", in *Equity in the World's Legal Systems*, 160 et seq.

of property, the equitable title, would be created and prevail in practice over legal property rights[50]. For the rest, this institution has survived until the present day in the Anglo-American legal tradition, though under the name of trust, due to the new slant that the Chancery had to give to its activity in order to elude the attack of the 1536 Statute of Uses.

Some historical evidence suggests that the birth of the English use was not alien to canon law. First, the use was created by the ecclesiastical Chancellors, and it is presumable that their concept of conscience was strongly influenced by canonical ideas[51]. Moreover, intervention by Chancery in cases involving uses was induced, to a large extent, by two factors. One is the purpose of evading the statutes of mortmain which, from 1279 (statute *De viris religiosis*), endeavored to prevent religious institutions from acquiring real property. The other is the expansion of the mendicant orders — especially the Franciscans — whose ownership of property was severely restricted by their own internal rules[52]. Furthermore, it appears to be true that uses were afforded a certain protection by the ecclesiastical courts before Chancery took them within its competence[53] (which in turn has brought into

---

[50] See S.W. De Vine, "The Concept of *epiekeia* in the Chancellor of England's Enforcement of the Feoffment to Uses before 1535", 21 *University of British Columbia Law Review* 323 et seq. (1987).

[51] This fact has been already analyzed, in dealing with the Court of Chancery: see chapter 4.2.

[52] See S. Raban, *Mortmain Legislation and the English Church, 1279-1500* (Cambridge, 1982); S.W. De Vine, "The Franciscan Friars, the Feoffment to Uses, and Canonical Theories of Property Enjoyment before 1535", 10 *The Journal of Legal History* 1 et seq. (1989); J.H. Baker, *An Introduction to English Legal History*, 207 et seq.; H.J. Berman, *Law and Revolution*, 239.

[53] See R.H. Helmholz, "The Early Enforcement of Uses", in *Canon Law and the Law of England*, 341 et seq.; S.F.C. Milsom, *Historical Foundations*, 200 et seq.

question the possible influence of the Roman *fideicommissum* on the English use[54]).

4. Law of Associations and Law of Bankruptcy

The list of areas where the evolution of the common law tradition has been influenced by canon law can now be rounded out with a brief reference to another two fields of English law: associations and bankruptcy.

In the chapter on constitutional law, I indicated that the notion of *persona ficta* — already present in the work of Sinibaldo Fieschi, in the thirteenth century — constituted the central point around which medieval canonists and civilians construed a theory of public and private corporations[55]. It is known that, subsequently, the concept of "legal personality" became the axis of the doctrine of mercantile law of associations developed by Italian scholars. On the Continent this branch of law finds its origins in the contribution of medieval canonists[56].

A similar influence is perceptible in the beginnings of the common law on corporations, which assimilated a considerable part of canonical doctrine and experience in regard to the "legal persons": social purposes, statutory norms, organisms of representation and expression, rules on decision-making by collegiate bodies, etc.[57] Furthermore, the

---

[54] For the moment, historians have been unable to provide an unanimous and definite answer to this question. See R.H. Helmholz, "The English Law of Wills and the ius commune, 1450-1640", in L. Bonfield, ed, *Marriage, Property and Succession* (Berlin, 1992), 316 et seq.

[55] See chapter 9.2.

[56] See H.J. Berman, *Law and Revolution*, 336 et seq. The North American scholar remarks that there was a close relationship between religion and mercantile societies at that time, and stresses the influence that the summary procedure of canon law established in the decretal *Sæpe contingit* (1306) had on the practice of mercantile courts of England, Italy, France and Germany.

[57] See F. Pollock / F.W. Maitland, *History of English Law*, vol. 1, 486 et seq.

development of the concept of *persona ficta* by the canon lawyers led to what has been called the "concession theory". This meant that corporations could come into existence only when there was a concession of legal personality from the public authority, in accordance with the principle *solus princeps fingit quod in rei veritate non est* (only the prince can devise what is not in the truth of the thing, i.e. what does not actually exist). The concession theory would be unreservedly received by the English lawyers and enthusiastically accepted in North America. Its imprint on Anglo-American corporate law would last for a long time, namely until the nineteenth century, when it would be replaced by the concept of freely available incorporation[58].

In relation to bankruptcy law, it is a widespread opinion that the legal regulation of bankruptcy emerged *ex novo* in England with the Tudors' legislation, initiated in 1542 and developed especially after 1571. However, an examination of the Church courts' records reveals, once again, that the overall picture of the history of English law can be obtained only by knowing what occurred in the realm of ecclesiastical jurisdiction.

In fact, Helmholz has shown that, long before royal legislation on bankruptcy was enacted, the ecclesiastical courts had faced the problem of insolvency within the framework of their competence over the law of succession[59]. Probate proceedings often brought to light the fact that a person had died without sufficient assets to meet his debts. This led the ecclesiastical courts to develop a machinery to confront these situations, including the principal features of bankruptcy procedure: declaration of the state of insolvency, collection and confiscation of the deceased's belongings, invalidation of fraudulent transactions by the deceased prior to his death, establishment of priorities among creditors, etc.

---

[58] See F.W. Maitland, introduction to O. Gierke, *Political Theories of the Middle Age*, xviii et seq.

[59] See R.H Helmholz, "Bankruptcy and Probate Jurisdiction before 1571", in *Canon law and the law of England*, 291 et seq.; and also, within the same collection of articles, "Canon Law and the English Common Law", 11 et seq.

With some minor differences, these characteristics are substantially present also in the sixteenth century royal laws on bankruptcy. It is not possible to determine the extent to which the canonical practice actually inspired the Tudor legislation. However, the significant analogies between them suggest that, also in this area, the common lawyers were able to benefit from this "alien" legal system which they knew well enough.

Conclusion

This book, in its different chapters, refers to the flow of legal concepts and institutions which, through the canon law, entered the British Isles from across the Channel. However, this exposition is not exhaustive, nor can it be. I must admit that this is an unfinished task. It is predictable that further historical research will continue to unearth new information and rectify the data we currently have. Where history is concerned, one can never pretend to have the last word.

I have endeavored to describe a panorama complete enough to establish a basic fact: the Anglo-American legal tradition has more elements in common with continental law than is frequently believed. Nobody doubts that the legal systems of the European continent have their deepest and strongest roots in the "learned law" developed by medieval scholars. What I have tried to demonstrate is that the learned laws, and particularly the canon law, have also played a very significant role in the historical evolution of English law.

It is true that much of the canonical influence did not occur strictly within the domain of the common law, and that most of it streamed through other channels. But we must not forget that the common law is not the sole source of English law, though in the long run it turned to be its principal unifying factor. For centuries, other independent branches of English law coexisted with the common law: especially — as has repeatedly been noted in the preceding chapters of this book — the law applied by the ecclesiastical courts, and the equity administered and developed by the Court of Chancery. To them, we should add that impelling force which makes possible the progress of any legal system — the thought of jurists, who, in England, did not remain ignorant of the ideas of their continental colleagues.

For those reasons, it seems accurate to affirm that the Anglo-American tradition did not emerge *ex nihilo*, simply as a result of the creativity of the common lawyers evidenced in the daily dialectic between bar and bench. On the contrary, it grew from a prolonged and complex historical process whereby the originality of the common law became fused with elements of Christian origin. There is nothing strange about this within the context of the western medieval society, so closely identified with the concept of Christendom. Actually the continental law experienced a similar and contemporary process, though through diverse itineraries. As we have seen, these Christian elements sometimes were specific norms or institutions of the Roman-canonical law, and at other times were general principles based on the notions of natural justice and equity which stood at the very center of the medieval legal world.

For Anglo-American jurists, the search for Roman and canonical roots in their system is, no doubt, of the greatest interest insofar as it serves to disclose or clarify their own historical identity. This is a natural interest, for only in the light of its historical background is it possible to achieve a profound understanding and appraisal of the present state of a legal system, and to predict the main lines of its future evolution. In this regard, the formative process of the common law tradition shows numerous points of confluence with the civil law tradition, namely those relating to their common elements of Christian-canonical origin. This fact is precisely the reason that the Anglo-American and the continental legal traditions can be considered as the two components — the two sides — of one and the same legal culture, which embraces the entire western world. It is probably also the reason they can communicate with each other, for they share an important "juridical vocabulary", an ensemble of common legal concepts.

However, research into the canonical origins of the common law tradition is useful also for canonists. There are some significant elements of classical canon law which have remained concealed under the weight of the codification movements that were brought on by rationalism, and have actually been better preserved within the realm of a judge-made law. In other words, when canonists try to unveil the imprint left by canon law on English law, they are looking back on the legal tradition to which they themselves are heirs — the classical canon law — and which has substantially contributed to shaping the western legal systems.

A well-known French scholar, commenting on the contributions of canon law to our legal culture, has written that classical canon law was like the melting pot for the diverse legacies of ancient European civilizations. The law of the Church assimilated — and transformed according to the Christian spirit — "the care of the poor and the oppressed which was characteristic of Judaism, the Roman passion for order and authority, the political and logical conceptions of Greek philosophy, the enthusiasm and scrupulousness of the Celts"[1]. It may be objected that this is perhaps a too sublime — though attractive — perception of the European legal history, for, besides the desire to mould society according to the Christian spirit, there were other factors within the ecclesiastical environment — certainly less spiritual — which impelled the penetration of canon law into the secular legal structures of the Middle Ages.

Whatever our personal evaluation of the fact may be, the important thing is that argument for the influence of canon law on the Anglo-American legal tradition rests upon irrefutable historical evidence. And it seems to me, this fact is also of significance from the point of view of comparative law, for it helps to show the permeability of legal systems.

Legal systems are not hermetic and incommunicable. On the contrary, when they come into contact with each other, a kind of decanting of influences is produced in both directions, by means of a spontaneous and often imperceptible process which could well be labeled "legal osmosis". Such a process requires an instrument, an occasion, and a cause.

---

[1] G. Le Bras, "Canon Law", in *The Legacy of the Middle Ages*, 361.

The instrument is primarily the scholarly study of law. A reciprocal influence between legal systems is an interchange of juridical ideas and experiences. It seems natural that, due to their broader intellectual horizons, legal scholars are usually endowed with greater sensibility towards ideas proceeding from foreign environments, and more readily realize the extent to which they may be applicable within their own milieu.

The occasion is provided by the presence of one legal system within or beside another, and this is something that admits of diverse possibilities. Historically it occurred frequently — as in England — through the simultaneous coexistence of distinct jurisdictions within the same territory, but it can also be the consequence of a human, economic, cultural, or political communication between nations, as is more likely to happen in our own time.

The cause is the factor which determines the specific measure of mutual influence between the legal systems. It depends on circumstances so varied that they are impossible to state definitely; among them we can include, for example, the different perfection of the legal systems in contact, the influence of consuetudinary norms, or the versatility of political conditions, both national and international.

Of course, the absorption of a foreign juridical experience has a limited reach and in no way entails that legal systems become depersonalized — quite the contrary, it is normally an enriching process for them. The subject of this essay constitutes an eloquent testimony of it, for the remarkable contribution of canon law does not contradict at all the singularity of the Anglo-American legal tradition.

The common lawyers created an admirable juridical construction based on heterogeneous components, some of them native and some of them of continental origin. The use of the latter does not lessen the merit of their achievement. Their work did not consist in imitation, but rather in transformation. They assimilated elements from outside, and creatively adapted them to a different legal reality. They are the authors of an original and unique system, which is the result of not logic but of history.

Index

MIX
Papier aus verantwortungsvollen Quellen
Paper from responsible sources
FSC® C105338

Printed by Libri Plureos GmbH
in Hamburg, Germany